CHARMING SMALL HOTEL GUIDES

Britain's
Most Distinctive
Bed & Breakfasts

CHARMING SMALL HOTEL GUIDES

Britain's
Most Distinctive
Bed & Breakfasts

Edited by Paul Wade & Kathy Arnold

DUNCAN PETERSEN

HUNTER
PUBLISHING

Editors   Paul Wade, Kathy Arnold
Art director   Mel Petersen
Editorial director Andrew Duncan
Maps   Christopher Foley

First published in Great Britain in 1999 by
Duncan Petersen Publishing Ltd,
31 Ceylon Road, London W14 OPY

Sales representation and distribution in the U.K. and Ireland by
Portfolio Books Limited
Unit 1C, West Ealing Business Centre
Alexandria Road
London W13 0NJ
Tel: 0181 579 7748

ISBN 1 872576 74 5

A CIP catalogue record for this book is available
from the British Library

AND

Published in the USA by
Hunter Publishing Inc.,
130 Campus Drive, Edison, N.J. 08818.
Tel (732) 225 1900 Fax (732) 417 0482

For details on hundreds of other travel guides and language
courses, visit Hunter's Web site at hunterpublishing.com

ISBN 1-55650-794-1

Film production by SX Composing DTP
Printed by Delo Tiskarna, Slovenija

Contents

Introduction

In this, the latest book in the *Charming Small Hotel Guides* series, we are responding to our readers demands. Having made a timely departure to assess the growing number of bed-and-breakfasts in France, we turn to the country that invented the bed-and-breakfast: Britain.

The idea of offering bed-and-breakfast began when farmers offered the independent traveller a warm welcome, a clean room and a hearty breakfast at a bargain price. This simple concept has been exported around the globe. In some countries, such as the USA, bed-and-breakfast has turned into an upmarket experience, with 'innkeepers' opening up their antiques-filled homes. In the past decade, the British have also recognized the appeal of offering quality hospitality in distinctive homes. While there are still thousands of admirable farmhouse operations, we have searched for bed-and-breakfasts in cities and villages, on moors and by lakes, on mountainsides and by the shore, all of which have a special quality.

Although they offer a bedroom, breakfast and, often nowadays, an evening meal, the owners are not professional hoteliers. Nevertheless, the best bed-and-breakfasts in Britain are as true to the *Charming Small Hotels* philosophy as any small hotel. Their rooms look like real bedrooms; meals are carefully prepared, using local produce; hosts take a genuine interest in their guests. Above all, the atmosphere is personal, the experience special. They even offer a sense of adventure for travellers who, by staying in a bed-and-breakfast, will discover corners of Britain that they would otherwise never find.

This is one of the few *independently inspected*, UK-originated, colour accommodation guides to charming and distinctive bed-and-breakfast places in Britain. Beware of imitators who do not admit on the cover that they accept payments from hotels for inclusion but only do so in small print on the inside pages. They say they are selective – but a quick comparison with this guide will prove that this is a hollow claim.

Selection process

Families open their doors to visitors for different reasons: some offer a couple of rooms when their children have grown up and left home; others regard it as a small business, operating with considerable style and imagination. Our inspectors drove thousands of miles all over Britain,

The inspectors
Our selection has been made after thorough research, personal recommendations and expert assessment by a small, trained team of inspectors chosen by the editors.
No bed-and-breakfast pays to be in this guide.

searching for the best at several price levels. They prodded mattresses, checked the bathrooms, listened for traffic noise, tasted local dishes and, most important of all, talked to hosts in order to discover whether they possessed the human touch essential for running a pleasant bed-and-breakfast. Scores failed these tests.

In the end, we found more than 250 which met our standards. Of each we can honestly say that we would be happy to spend the night there. That, however, does not mean that they are all faultless.

We believe it is important to 'tell it like it is', so that readers can decide what will suit them best, for an overnight stop, a weekend break or a holiday by the sea. So, we spell out what is on offer: whether bedrooms are in the owners' house or in a separate building; whether the evening meal is value for money; whether children are welcome and pets accepted. If you read a note of criticism, it does not mean a bed-and-breakfast is not worth considering.

Size

In the main, our selections have between three and five bedrooms. In the countryside, outbuildings are often imaginatively converted into guest rooms, offering more privacy.

Facilities

Many have a swimming-pool or tennis court, with bicycles for guests to borrow or to hire. There may be a sitting-room where guests relax or a kitchen for preparing simple meals.

Bedrooms

Rooms vary in size and furnishings. Some have grand four-poster beds, others are suited to families, with extra beds for children. Our inspectors were impressed by the quality, particularly when compared with hotels or chain motels.

Bathrooms

British bathrooms have improved dramatically and often feature the power showers North Americans demand.

Most of the selections in this guide have an en suite bathroom and WC accessible directly from each guest bedroom. However, as many homes are centuries old, en suite bathrooms are not always architecturally feasible. A private bathroom is never more than a few steps from the bedroom, and rarely, if ever, shared by another couple.

Privacy

As almost all the entries are private homes, it is important to recognize the privacy of the hosts. Since these are not hotels, it is generally not appropriate for guests to be in their rooms or in the sitting-room all day long. Similarly, formal gardens, swimming-pools and tennis courts were created for the pleasure of the hosts. Please ask if it is convenient to use them.

Evening meals

Many hosts now offer an evening meal. This may be served at separate tables, or guests may gather round one large table. Sometimes hosts join guests at the table; at other times they are too busy serving to chat until after the meal.

Credit cards

Credit cards are not universally accepted by bed-and-breakfasts. Eurocheques and travellers' cheques are usually welcome but it is always advisable to double-check when booking your accommodation. Occasionally a credit card may be used to secure a reservation.

Stopovers and holidays

Hosts often offer reductions on longer stays. However, some owners insist on a minimum two-night stays.

Electricity

Do not expect to find international sockets. Be sure to take whatever adapter is necessary for your electric razor or hairdrier. Hairdriers are usually available.

How this guide is organized

Entries are arranged geographically. England, Scotland and Wales are divided into 10 regions.

Maps

Each area has its own map (*pages 11–31*) with a nearby town as a locator to help find the bed-and-breakfasts which are often off the beaten track. A page reference helps you find the entry.

Entries

The major entries appear in the front of the book, each with a colour photograph. These are our warmest recommendations.

At the back of the book are shorter entries, four to a page. These are by no means 'second-class' bed-and-breakfasts. They give readers more options, different experiences. Some may have only two rooms, others are heavily booked, still others are difficult to get to. Nevertheless, we are enthusiastic about **all** of them.

How to find an entry

There are three easy ways to find a bed-and-breakfast:

1 Use the maps on pages 11 to 31. The numbers on the

map refer to the page in the guide where the bed-and-breakfast is listed. **2** If you know the area you want to visit, browse through that section until you find a place that fits the bill. Or **3** use the index at the back which lists entries by their location (p187–190).

How to read an entry

At the top of the page is a small map highlighting the region of Britain covered on that page. Below that is the region, then the town or village with a directional 'locator' eg E of Bath (east of Bath) as an orientation point on the map. **We strongly advise using a large scale road atlas.** Finally, the name of the house itself.

Fact boxes

Beneath each bed-and-breakfast description are facts and figures that should help you to decide whether it is within your price range and has the facilities you require.

Tel

Calling from abroad, dial 44 for Britain, but drop the 0 at the beginning of the number. Avoid calling at breakfast or in the evening. These are private homes, not hotels.

Fax and e-mail

It is good practice to confirm a telephone booking in writing, and several enterprising hosts also now use e-mail.

Prices

The range of prices are **per person, based on two sharing a room, with breakfast.** While a few entries have single rooms, one person using a double room has to pay a premium. Ask about discounts for longer stays.

up to	£20	£
	£20–£27	££
	£27–£35	£££
	over £35	££££

Evening meal

Some hosts do not offer dinner, since there are often eating places nearby. 'By request only' indicates those who do, but guests **must give their hosts advance warning.** The evening meal can vary in price from £10 for supper to as much as £25 per head for a formal meal. Where these are well-priced, we say so in the text. **DB&B** indicates that dinner is included in the price.

Rooms

Bedrooms come in all shapes and sizes, grand and

Introduction

Georgian, snug and cottagey. We have categorized them as **double** or **single**. This merely means a room for two or a room for one. Some rooms have double beds, others are twin bedded. The twins can sometimes be zipped together to make a double. If you insist on a double or twin bed, ask your host. All houses listed have proper heating.

Credit cards
We use the following abbreviations for credit cards:

AE	American Express
DC	Diners Club
MC	Master Card/Access/Eurocard
V	Visa/Barclaycard/Bank Americard/Carte Bleue

Children
Children are welcome in most bed-and-breakfasts. In some, the rooms are not large enough for a cot or roll-away bed, so a separate room has to be booked. This will almost always be true once a child reaches 12 years of age.

Disabled
Most owners are willing to help but few homes are adapted for wheelchairs, especially the bathrooms. Some, however, have bedrooms on the ground floor. Discuss individual needs by telephone beforehand with the owner.

Pets
Most hosts have a dog or a cat. If guests' pets are welcomed, they are seldom allowed to sleep in the bedroom, since this would be unfair on subsequent guests.

Closed
Do double-check the exact dates of closing. Even those hosts who say they never close may decide to take a break in winter.

Languages
More and more hosts speak a foreign language, but those who don't are still likely to be as helpful as possible.

Proprietors
Occasionally, a manager or housekeeper will help a family with a large house.

And finally ....
We cannot stress enough how necessary it is to telephone hosts ahead of time. The best homes are the most popular, even 'out of season'. Moreover, where hotels are usually in towns, many bed-and-breakfasts are deep in the country-side, off the beaten track.

Location maps

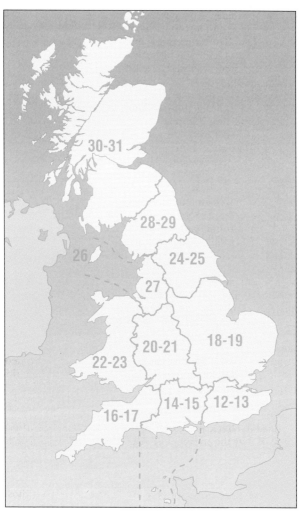

SOUTHERN ENGLAND
London and the South-East 12-13
The South and Channel Islands 14-15
The South-West 16-17

CENTRAL ENGLAND
East Anglia and the East Midlands 18-19
The Cotswolds and the Midlands 20-21

WALES 22-23

NORTHERN ENGLAND
Yorkshire 24-25
The North-West 26-27
The Lake District and the North 28-29

SCOTLAND 30-31

11

London and The South-East

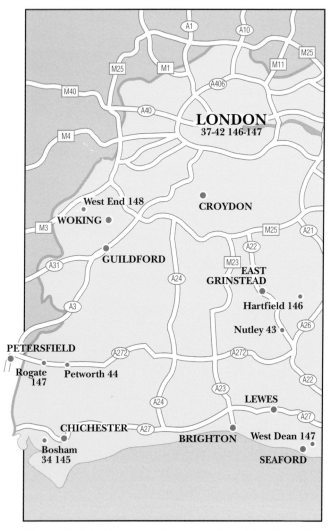

Most of Britain's visitors enter the country through London or the South-East. Although the capital has hundreds of bed-and-breakfasts, we feature only a handful of owners who match our exacting standards. A number of first-class London bed-and-breakfasts prefer to maintain their anonymity by joining central reservation services. Their standards will depend on the criteria of the person running the consortium. We are impressed by small companies such as At Home in London (0181 748 1943), where all the properties are inspected by organiser Maggie Dobson.

Our selection in the South-East, which includes the counties of Kent, Sussex and Surrey, includes some of the country's most delightful places to stay in some of England's prettiest countryside,

London and The South-East

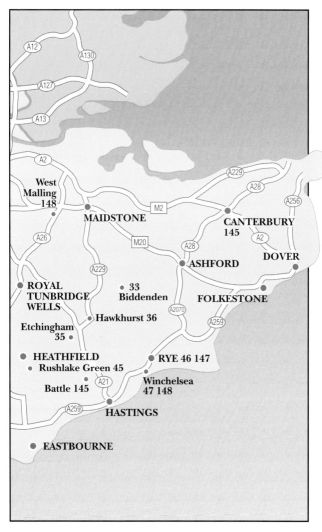

but there are also outstanding properties in historic seaside towns such as Rye and Winchelsea.

For more information on the region contact:

London Tourist Board
6th Floor
Glen House, Stag Place,
London SW1E 5LT
Tel: 0171 932 2000
Fax: 0171 932 0222
www.LondonTown.com

South East England Tourist
Board
The Old Brew House
Warwick Park
Tunbridge Wells
Kent TN2 5TU
Tel: 01892 540766
Fax: 01892 511008
www.seetb.org.uk

The South and Channel Islands

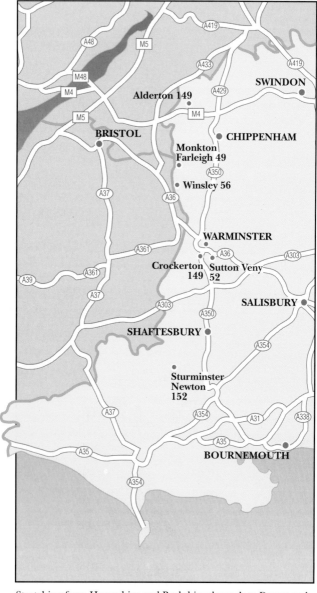

Stretching from Hampshire and Berkshire through to Dorset and Wiltshire, this is another area full of beauty spots and fine old country towns and cities such as Winchester and Salisbury. Our inspectors found waterside cottages and houses on the River Thames and the Test, as well as appealingly eccentric places where the expression 'getting away from it all' really does ring true.

The South and Channel Islands

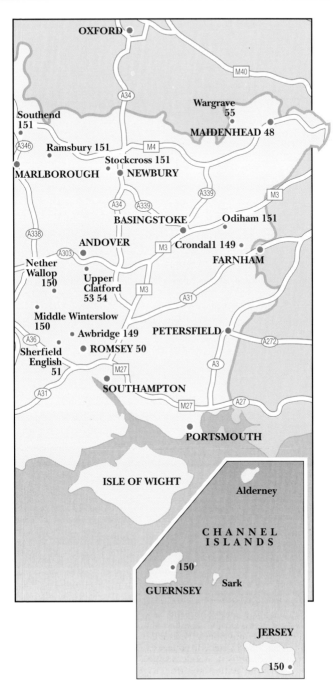

OXFORD

M40

A34

Wargrave
55

Southend
151

MAIDENHEAD 48

A346

Ramsbury 151

M4

Stockcross 151

MARLBOROUGH

NEWBURY

A339

M3

A34   A339

BASINGSTOKE

Odiham 151

A338

ANDOVER

Crondal1 149

A303

M3

FARNHAM

Nether
Wallop
150

Upper
Clatford
53 54

M3

A31

Middle Winterslow
150

A36

Awbridge 149

PETERSFIELD

A272

Sherfield
English
51

ROMSEY 50

A3

M27

A31

SOUTHAMPTON

M27   A27

PORTSMOUTH

ISLE OF WIGHT

Alderney

C H A N N E L
I S L A N D S

150

Sark

GUERNSEY

JERSEY

150

The South-West

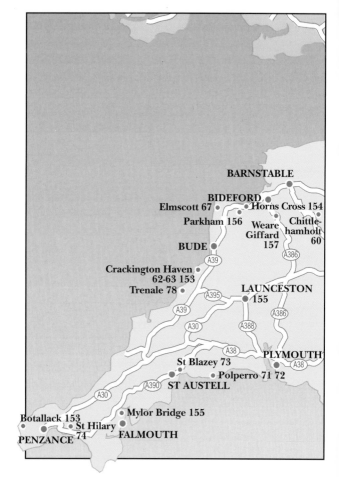

BARNSTABLE

BIDEFORD
Elmscott 67 • • Horns Cross 154
Parkham 156 Weare Chittle-
Giffard hamholt
BUDE • 157 60

Crackington Haven •
62-63 153
Trenale 78 • LAUNCESTON
155

PLYMOUTH

St Blazey 73
• Polperro 71 72
ST AUSTELL

Botallack 153 • Mylor Bridge 155
• St Hilary •
PENZANCE 74 FALMOUTH

This part of England has long been a favourite holiday destination
for the British themselves. As well as the seaside resorts and fishing
villages, there are the rolling hills of Devon with deep lanes and
bleak moors, the rocky shores of Cornwall and the mellow
countryside of Somerset. And then there is the famous city of
Bath. The concept of bed-and-breakfast could well have developed
in this part of England, and we are happy to report that there are
many high-quality places to stay, where the standards rival those of
many small hotels in the region. In Bath and the smaller country
towns, there is not only comfortable accommodation, but also
hosts who can add an extra dimension to a holiday through their
own knowledge of the local attractions.

The South-West

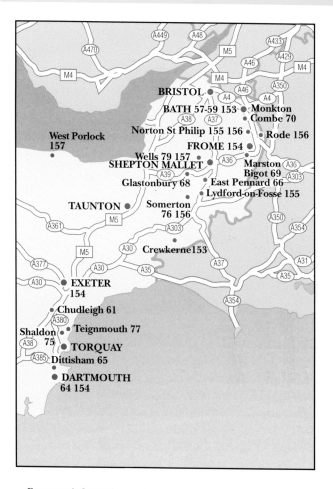

For more information on the region contact:

West Country Tourist Board
60 St David's Hill
Exeter
EX4 4SY
Tel: 01392 425436
Fax: 01392 420891
www.wctb.co.uk

East Anglia and The East Midlands

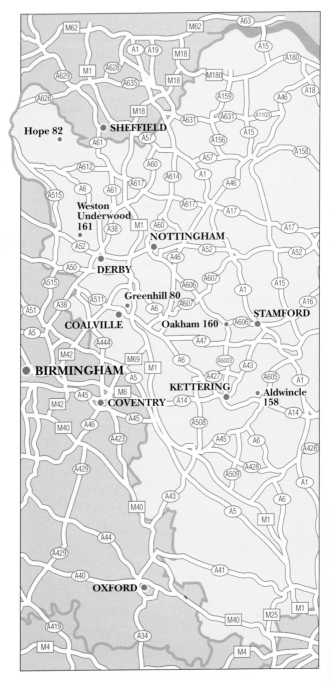

East Anglia and The East Midlands

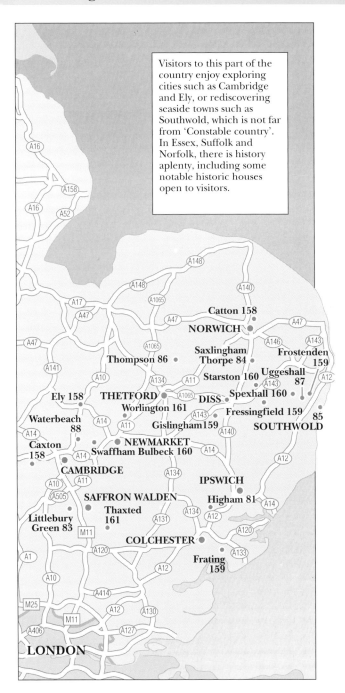

Visitors to this part of the country enjoy exploring cities such as Cambridge and Ely, or rediscovering seaside towns such as Southwold, which is not far from 'Constable country'. In Essex, Suffolk and Norfolk, there is history aplenty, including some notable historic houses open to visitors.

Catton 158

NORWICH

Saxlingham
Thorpe 84

Frostenden
159

Thompson 86

Uggeshall
87

Starston 160

Spexhall 160

THETFORD

DISS

Worlington 161

Fressingfield 159

Ely 158

85

Gislingham 159

SOUTHWOLD

Waterbeach
88

NEWMARKET

Caxton
158

Swaffham Bulbeck 160

CAMBRIDGE

IPSWICH

SAFFRON WALDEN

Higham 81

Thaxted
161

Littlebury
Green 83

COLCHESTER

Frating
159

LONDON

The Cotswolds and The Midlands

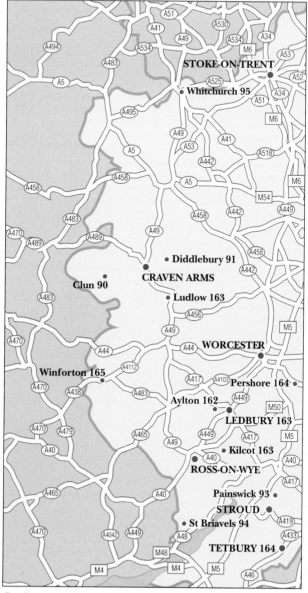

Our inspectors found some very good bed-and-breakfasts in well-known villages such as Broadway, as well as in unassuming hamlets such as Clun and St Briavels. Book well ahead if you are planning to visit a popular spot in the Cotswolds.

The Cotswolds and The Midlands

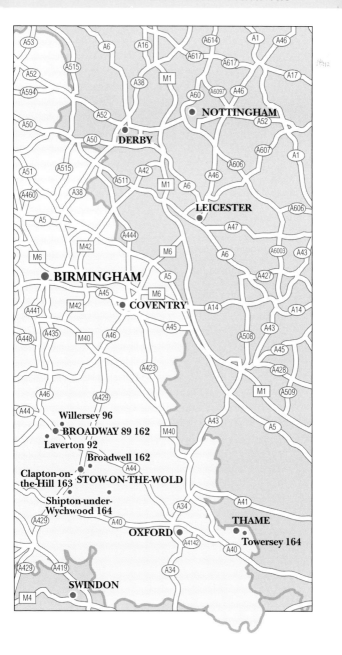

Wales

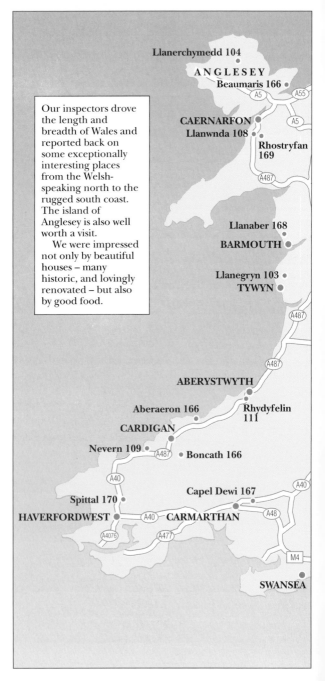

Our inspectors drove the length and breadth of Wales and reported back on some exceptionally interesting places from the Welsh-speaking north to the rugged south coast. The island of Anglesey is also well worth a visit.

We were impressed not only by beautiful houses – many historic, and lovingly renovated – but also by good food.

Llanerchymedd 104

ANGLESEY
Beaumaris 166

CAERNARFON
Llanwnda 108

Rhostryfan 169

Llanaber 168
BARMOUTH

Llanegryn 103
TYWYN

ABERYSTWYTH

Aberaeron 166
Rhydyfelin 111

CARDIGAN

Nevern 109
Boncath 166

Capel Dewi 167

Spittal 170
HAVERFORDWEST
CARMARTHAN

SWANSEA

Wales

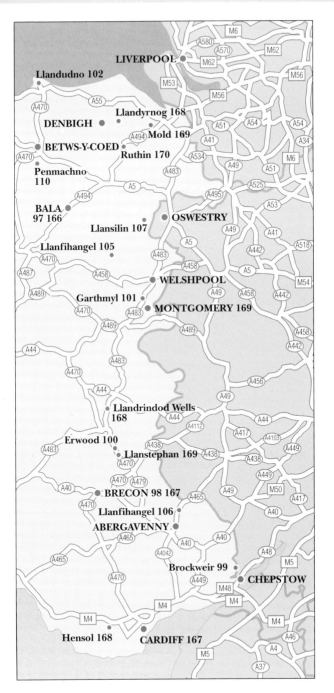

Yorkshire

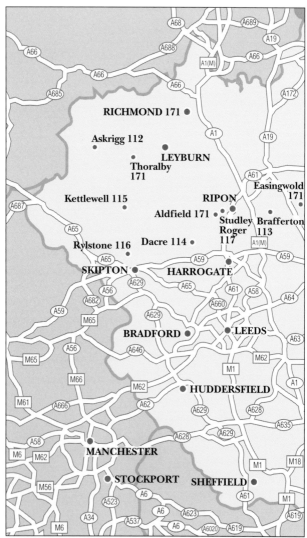

Despite the political interventions of recent decades, Yorkshire is still a distinctive entity, with a wide range of landscapes and attractions together with interesting cities such as York and handsome market towns such as Richmond. Our inspectors found practical accommodation in the cities and unexpected grandeur in the country, near romantic ruins such as Fountains Abbey. It almost goes without saying that breakfasts are hearty and generous.

However, we'd be interested in more reports from this region on outstanding places that could be suitable for this guide. Please see page 32.

Yorkshire

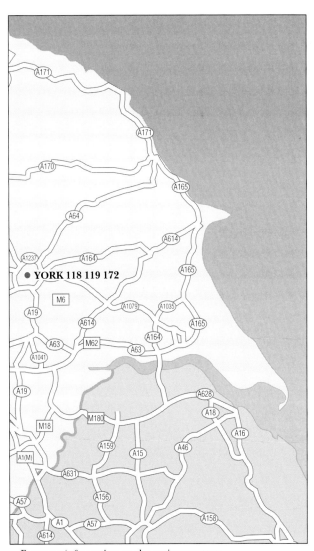

For more information on the region contact:

Yorkshire Tourist Board
312 Tadcaster Road
York
YO2 2HY
Tel: 01904 701100
Fax: 01904 701414
www.ytb.org.uk

The North-West

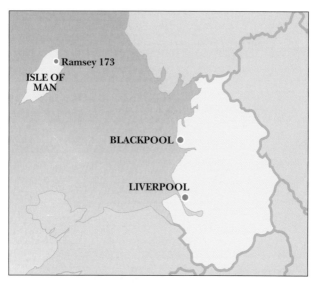

This is just a small corner of England, including Cheshire with its charming city of Chester and the countryside to the north-west of Manchester and its sprawling conurbations. The Isle of Man is crammed with bed-and-breakfasts, but we would welcome reports on exceptional ones.

For more information on the region contact:

North West Tourist Board
Swan House
Swan Meadow Road
Wigan Pier
Wigan, Lancs
WN3 5BB
Tel: 01942 821222
Fax: 01942 820002
www.visitbritain.com

The Isle of Man Tourism
Sea Terminal Buildings
Douglas
Isle of Man
IM1 2RG
Tel: 01624 686760
Fax: 01624 686800
www.gov.im/tourism

The North-West

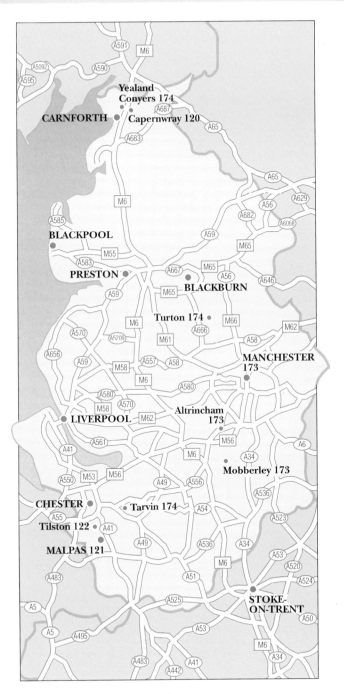

The Lake District and The North

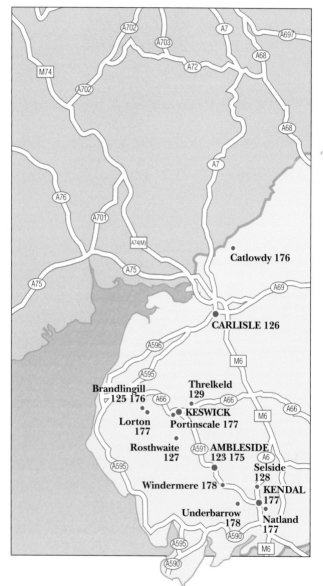

Along with the Cotswolds, the Lake District must be the most-visited locality of England. Only a handful of houses live up to expectations, but the best will offer you tips on how to avoid the crowds and tour buses, and where to get good food. Don't miss the area to the north and east of the lakes, along the Scottish borders, where houses may be less grand, but where the comfort and welcome is just as enthusiastic.

The Lake District and The North

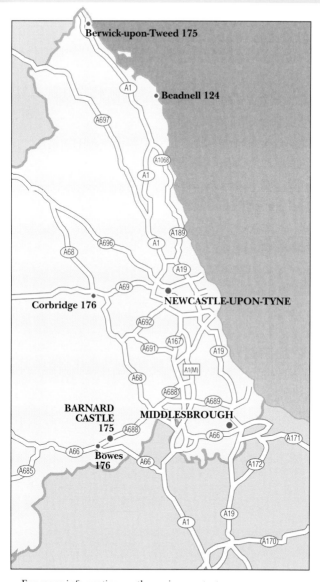

For more information on the region contact:

Cumbria Tourist Board
Ashleigh
Holly Road
Windermere
Cumbria
LA23 2AQ
Tel: 015394 44444
Fax: 015394 44041
www.cumbria-the-lake-district.co.uk

Northumbria Tourist Board
Aykley Heads
Durham
DH1 5UX
Tel: 0191 375 3000
Fax: 0191 386 0899
www.northumbria.tourist-board.org.uk

Scotland

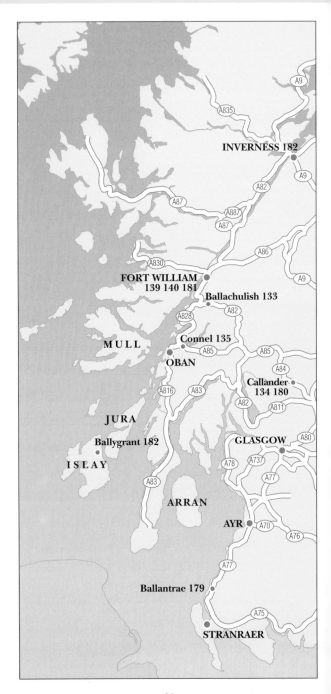

Scotland

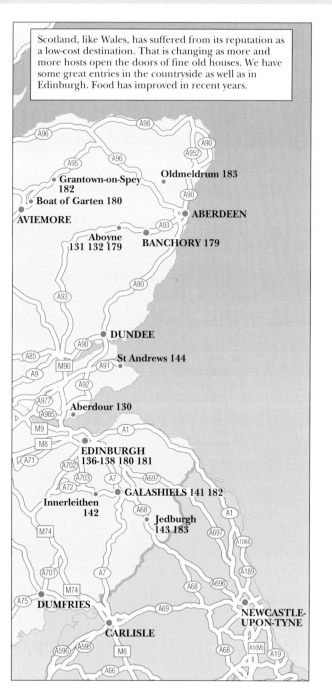

Scotland, like Wales, has suffered from its reputation as a low-cost destination. That is changing as more and more hosts open the doors of fine old houses. We have some great entries in the countryside as well as in Edinburgh. Food has improved in recent years.

Grantown-on-Spey 182

Oldmeldrum 183

Boat of Garten 180

AVIEMORE

ABERDEEN

Aboyne 131 132 179

BANCHORY 179

DUNDEE

St Andrews 144

Aberdour 130

EDINBURGH 136-138 180 181

GALASHIELS 141 182

Innerleithen 142

Jedburgh 143 183

DUMFRIES

CARLISLE

NEWCASTLE-UPON-TYNE

Reporting to the guide

Please write and tell us about your experiences of small hotels, bed-and-breakfasts and inns, whether good or bad, whether listed in this edition or not. As well as bed-and-breakfasts in Britain, we are interested in charming small hotels in: Britain, Ireland, Italy, France, Spain, Portugal, Germany, Austria, Switzerland and other European countries, as well as New England, Florida, and the west coast of the United States.

The address to write to is:
The Editors
Britain's Most Distinctive Bed-and-Breakfasts
Charming Small Hotel Guides
Duncan Petersen Publishing Ltd.
31 Ceylon Road
London W14 0PY
England

Checklist
Please use a separate sheet of paper for each report; include your name, address and telephone number on each report. Your reports will be received with particular pleasure if they are typed, and if they are organized under the following headings:

    Name of establishment
    Town or village it is in, or nearest
    Full address, including postcode
    Telephone number
    Time and duration of visit
    The building and setting
    The public rooms
    The bedrooms and bathrooms
    Physical comfort (chairs, beds, heat, light, hot water)
    Standards of maintenance and housekeeping
    Atmosphere, welcome and service
    Food
    Value for money

We assume that in writing you have no objection to your views being published unpaid, either verbatim or in an edited version. Names of major outside contributors are acknowledged in the guide, at the editors' discretion.

London and The South-East

Biddenden, SE of Maidstone

Bishopsdale Oast

Bishopsdale Oast is one of dozens of oast houses, whose conical towers punctuate the rolling, fertile countryside of Kent. Built for drying the hops used in making beer, many have now been converted to homes. This one worked from the mid-18thC until 1963, which was a bumper year, according to the record-board in the hallway. Now, the original fireplace is in the guest sitting-room, while the room above, where the hops were spread out to dry, is the largest of the three bedrooms. Another bedroom, on the ground floor, opens on to a corner of the garden.

Owner Jane Drysdale is a professional caterer, so four-course dinners here are above average, featuring vegetables from the garden and English cheeses. Although Jane makes the plum and strawberry jams, her husband, Iain, is the breakfast chef. In fine weather, meals are served on the west-facing terrace, by the croquet lawn and wildflower meadow. Set deep in the countryside, yet close to castles, gardens and charming villages, its informal atmosphere and creature comforts make this a fine example of the new breed of British bed-and-breakfasts.

Nearby Sissinghurst, Leeds and Bodiam Castles, vineyards.
Directions 16 miles SE of Maidstone. Get final directions.

Biddenden, Kent TN27 8DR
Tel (01580) 291027
Fax (01580) 292321
Location in deep countryside; ample car parking
Evening meal by request
Prices £££
Rooms 3 double; all have TV, radio, tea/coffee kit
Facilities sitting-room, dining-room; garden
Smoking restricted
Credit cards MC, V
Children over 10

Disabled not suitable
Pets no
Closed Christmas
Languages French, some Italian
Proprietors Jane and Iain Drysdale a

London and The South-East

Critchfield House

What do visitors want in a bed-and-breakfast? Before opening to guests, Janetta Field slept in each of her bedrooms and asked herself what she would like to find there. The result is light-switches that can be reached from beds, and trays with tea and coffee, as well as herbal teas, hot chocolate, fresh fruit and biscuits, all set out on pretty white china. She also put proper shower cabinets in the bathrooms and decorated in spring-like greens and yellows. Breakfast is taken together at a massive antique table in the oak-beamed dining room. According to one enthusiastic and carnivorous guest, it is 'scrumptious, with special sausages made for 90 years by Elphick's of Chichester'. There are also home-made jams and breads for vegetarians. Mrs Field does not offer dinner, but a hotel and pubs are a stroll away. Book well ahead during Chichester's theatre season.

As for Old Bosham itself, this 'jewel of a village' right on the water attracts artists who paint the 18thC houses plus the church, which dates back over 900 years.

Nearby Chichester and its cathedral, Goodwood House.
Directions 4 miles W of Chichester. Take A259 to Bosham. House is in the middle of the village, next to a garage.

Bosham Lane, Old Bosham, West Sussex PO18 8HG
Tel and Fax (01243) 572370
Location in heart of village; ample car parking
Evening meal no
Prices ££
Rooms 4 double; all have TV, radio, hairdrier, tea/coffee kit
Facilities dining-room; walled garden, terrace
Smoking outdoors only
Credit cards no

Children welcome
Disabled not suitable
Pets by arrangement
Closed Nov to Feb
Languages English only
Proprietor Janetta Field

London and The South-East

Etchingham, SE of Royal Tunbridge Wells

King John's Lodge

'Quintessentially English' was the reaction of our globe-trotting inspector, who was as fascinated by the gardens as by the house. Start with the house, which dates back to 1300 and is a 'compare and contrast' lesson in Elizabethan, Jacobean, Victorian and Edwardian architecture. Students should note the huge inglenook fireplace, massive oak beams and stairs that climb straight past a brick chimney.

The garden, too, is a showpiece, though in 1987 when Jill and Richard Cunningham bought the Lodge it was totally overgrown. Now, it is sometimes open to the public, who stroll through the 'wild garden', with its cow-parsley and black tulips, then admire the ha-ha, a banked ditch that keeps the sheep in their meadow and away from the lawn. Inside, bedrooms come in different sizes; some bathrooms are fitted into cramped spaces. Who cares, when you could sleep where King John of France slept? Legend says that he was held prisoner here in the 14thC.

Nearby Bodiam Castle, Rudyard Kipling home, gardens.

Directions 11 miles SE of Royal Tunbridge Wells. Take A21 for Hastings; at Hurst Green, take A265 to Etchingham. House 1 mile from village. Get final directions.

Sheepstreet Lane, Etchingham, East Sussex TN19 7AZ	**Smoking** restricted
Tel (01580) 819232	**Credit cards** no
Fax (01580) 819562	**Children** over 10
Location on country lane; ample car parking	**Disabled** not suitable
Evening meal by request	**Pets** yes
Prices ££–£££	**Closed** Christmas, New Year
Rooms 3 double; all have tea/coffee kit	**Languages** English only
Facilities 2 sitting-rooms, dining-room; terrace, garden, croquet, tennis court	**Proprietors** Jill and Richard Cunningham

London and The South-East

Hawkhurst, SE of Royal Tunbridge Wells

Conghurst Farm

Richard Piper's roots go deep into the fertile soil of Kent. The records in the local church trace the Piper name back to 1760, but his forebears were here long before William the Conqueror. His family have lived on this land since 900.

From this spot, there are no roads, railway or power lines to spoil the view across the valley and into the hills of Sussex. The house itself is full of intriguing fragments of history, such as the marriage crest symbolizing the union of two families back in Tudor times. The newest rooms are the drawing-room and dining-room, dating from 1829. Despite their handsome proportions and antique furnishings, we found the overall ambience informal and relaxing. Rosemary Piper is determined to keep it that way. "After all, this is still a family home and a working farm, not a hotel." Bedrooms upstairs are fresh-looking but not expensively furnished. This is reflected in the sensible prices. Also sensible is the decision to offer a two-course supper on weekdays, saving the special three-course dinner for weekends.

Nearby Scotney and Bodiam castles, Great Dixter gardens.
Directions 10 miles SE of Royal Tunbridge Wells. Take A21 for Hastings, then A268 for Hawkhurst. Get final directions.

Hawkhurst, Kent TN18 4RW	**Children** over 12
Tel (01580) 753331	**Disabled** not suitable
Fax (01580) 754579	**Pets** no
Location in deep countryside; ample car parking	**Closed** Dec, Jan
	Languages English only
Evening meal by request	**Proprietor** Rosemary Piper
Prices ££	
Rooms 3 double; all have TV, radio, hairdrier, tea/coffee kit	
Facilities 2 sitting-rooms, dining-room; garden	
Smoking outdoors only	
Credit cards no	

London and The South-East

London

30 King Henry's Road

The Ingrams used to live in the country, but are now enthusiastic about London and its attractions. 'We want visitors to get the most out of their stay,' says Carole Ingram, who has tips for getting theatre tickets or jumping the queues to visit Buckingham Palace. Their imposing five-storey home is near an Underground station, handy for Central London.

Carole's flair as an interior decorator shows when you enter the grand hallway, its walls smothered in pictures. Brightly-coloured pottery vases and platters line up to do battle with books for space on the shelves. This is the Ingrams' home, so 'we don't have keys for the doors. We could not live like that.' The bedrooms have character with brass beds, antique chests-of-drawers and down pillows. At the top of steep stairs, the two rooms at the rear each have a private bathroom across the hall, as well as air-conditioning. Although they face a main railway line, the occasional train horn is not intrusive. Breakfast, with home-made preserves, is at a table in the rustic chic kitchen, crammed with more pottery and dried flowers.

Nearby London Zoo, Central London.
Directions 5 minutes' walk from Chalk Farm Underground.

---

30 King Henry's Road,
London NW3 3RP
Tel (0171) 483 2871
Fax (0171) 483 4587
Location on quiet residential road; street car parking
Evening meal no
Prices ££££
Rooms 3 double; all have TV, radio, hairdrier
Facilities sitting-room; garden
Smoking outdoors only
Credit cards no
Children welcome

Disabled not suitable
Pets by arrangement
Closed never
Languages French
Proprietors Carole and Andrew Ingram

London and The South-East

London

47 Warwick Gardens

The area of west London around Earl's Court and West Kensington is residential but punctuated with small hotels. Most accommodation is highly commercial, so this large 1840 town-house is a find. There are no signs outside, no stickers in the windows, as this really is a family home. Owner Nanette Stylianou, who is French, bubbles with enthusiasm. With a background in the luxury hotel business, she has all the attributes of an accomplished hostess. Her sitting-room, which opens into the dining-room, is stylish and grand. By contrast, her bedrooms and bathrooms are plain, practical and, by North American standards, a little small. All, however, look fresh and bright. Although the larger bedrooms are at the front, two at the back open on to a patio and garden, where purple clematis climbs the walls and tall trees block off the houses beyond.

Although Warwick Gardens is a busy street during the day, a barrier shuts it off to vehicles between 11pm and 6am, so traffic noise is not a problem. With Underground stations nearby, this is an elegant and convenient place to stay, at a reasonable price.

Nearby Kensington High Street, Holland Park, shopping.
Directions nearest Underground station, Earl's Court.

47 Warwick Gardens, London
W14 8PL
Tel (0171) 603 7614
Fax (0171) 602 5473
E-mail sstyla@aol.com
Location on one-way street; private car parking
Evening meal no
Prices ££££
Rooms 4 double; all have TV, hairdrier, tea/coffee kit
Facilities sitting-room, dining-room; garden
Smoking outdoors only

Credit cards no
Children over 12
Disabled not suitable
Pets no
Closed never
Languages French, some German, Italian
Proprietor Nanette Stylianou

London and The South-East

London

Aster House

Summer Place, tucked around the corner from South Kensington Underground station, is close to shops, restaurants and museums. In this short street, almost all the houses are now hotels. Aster House, festooned with flowers, has long offered value for money. In 1997, a new company took over, with Simon Tan as the manager. He is overseeing a much-needed programme of redecoration and rebuilding. Bedrooms, which previously offered minimal extras, now have direct-dial telephones, toiletries and tea and coffee kits. Although rooms are small even by city standards, plans are in hand to gradually upgrade throughout. Two at the back have been expanded, while the Four Poster Room at the front is in constant demand. We only hope the new owners can keep their promise to keep prices competitive.

Apart from the grandiose figures holding chandeliers in the hallway, the most striking feature of the Aster is the conservatory filled with plants. With its green tablecloths and pink chairs, this is a cheerful place to start the day. Breakfasts have been improved, offering more variety, catering for international tastes.

Nearby museums, Royal Albert Hall, Harrods.

Directions 3 minutes walk to South Kensington Underground.

3 Sumner Place, London
SW7 3EE
Tel (0171) 581 5888
Fax (0171) 584 4925
E-mail asterhouse@btinternet.com
Location on residential street;
public car parking
Evening meal no
Prices ££££
Rooms 10 double; 2 single; all
have telephone, TV, radio,
tea/coffee kit
Facilities breakfast room
Smoking restricted

Credit cards MC, V
Children welcome
Disabled not suitable
Pets no
Closed never
Languages Chinese
Manager Simon Tan

London and The South-East

Durley House

Durley House is neither a hotel nor a traditional bed-and-breakfast, but we happily recommend it to those seeking privacy and luxury. There are just a dozen suites, all furnished with antiques and lined with oil paintings and watercolours. One suite has a baby grand piano; all have small kitchens which, as well as standard bar items, even have a selection of wines in the racks. Bathrooms are marbled, bedrooms indulgent. Yet the sofas and stuffed armchairs are 'the sort where you can put your feet up and watch TV,' according to an American who likes to bring his family along on business trips. Each morning, a table is laid specially for breakfast, served whenever guests want.

All this is hidden behind a Georgian-style façade, on Sloane Street, in London's most fashionable shopping area. Guests come and go as they please, ringing the buzzer for entry. Some wear *haute couture*, others jeans. All have access to Cadogan Gardens, with its tennis courts. The most expensive place in this book, this is a regular haunt for the affluent, but could be a special occasion hideaway for ordinary mortals.

Nearby Harrods, Knightsbridge, Sloane Square, Hyde Park.
Directions nearest Underground station, Sloane Square.

115 Sloane Street, London
SW1X 9PJ
Tel (0171) 235 5537; USA 1-800 553 6674
Fax (0171) 259 6977
E-mail durley@firmdale.com
Location on main street; secure public car parking
Evening meal by request
Prices ££££
Rooms 11 suites; all have telephone, TV, radio, hairdrier, tea/coffee kit, fax machine, kitchen, 24-hour room service
Facilities sitting-room; garden
Smoking permitted
Credit cards AE, MC, V
Children very welcome
Disabled not suitable
Pets no
Closed never
Languages French, German, Italian, Spanish, Korean
Proprietors The Small Hotel Company

London and The South-East

London

Leyden House

Few private houses look right on to the River Thames, and this is the only one we know that opens its doors to guests. The view north is over a bend in the river, to a boathouse and a massive pole that marks the finish of the annual Oxford versus Cambridge University boat race. Apart from that one boisterous day in spring, this is a peaceful area, unknown even to most Londoners.

Painted a cheerful butter-yellow, with twin staircases guarded by twin stone lions, Leyden House is a large, mainly Georgian mansion. As owner Mrs Keeling admits, 'it works very well for guests, as they have their own floor with their own sitting-room.' This is where the television, tea and coffee kit, irons and hairdriers are kept. We like the Yellow Bedroom, with its two dormer windows looking on to the water. Like the other rooms, it is full of memorabilia, old prints and pictures from the family's travels around the world. Bathrooms are well-equipped with powerful showers. Most guests leave their cars here and go by bus or train to Central London.

Nearby Kew Gardens, Hampton Court, Richmond.
Directions near Chiswick Bridge. Get final directions.

Thames Bank, London
SW14 7QR
Tel (0181) 876 7375
Fax (0181) 876 6188
Location overlooking River Thames; public and private car parking
Evening meal no
Prices ££££
Rooms 2 double; 1 single
Facilities sitting-room, dining-room; garden, heated outdoor swimming-pool
Smoking outdoors only

Credit cards no
Children over 12
Disabled not suitable
Pets no
Closed never
Languages some French, German
Proprietor Mrs Rachael Keeling

London and The South-East

Searcy's Roof Garden Bedrooms

For 150 years, Searcy's has been synonymous with grand London parties. Almost unknown is this catering company's collection of rooms, a stone's throw from the world-famous shops of Knightsbridge and Sloane Street. As he stepped out of the old-fashioned lift straight on to the street, our inspector summed it all up in one word: eccentric.

The bottom half of the building hosts functions such as wedding receptions; upstairs are 11 bedrooms, including three singles. Once guests have their key, they come and go as they please, using the private entrance. Corridors are narrow and bedrooms are small, with surprisingly dated fabrics, wallpaper and beige carpets. A much-needed programme of repainting and renovation was carried out in the summer of 1997. The eccentricity comes with the arrangement of beds and baths. One twin room has the beds set into an alcove along one wall; other rooms have the bath in the bedroom itself. For the area, the prices and comfort are acceptable as long as housekeeping standards are retained. A light breakfast is delivered to the room.

Nearby Harrods, Knightsbridge, Sloane Street, Hyde Park.
Directions nearest Underground station, Knightsbridge.

30 Pavilion Road,
Knightsbridge, London
SW1X 0HJ
Tel (0171) 584 4921
Fax (0171) 823 8694
Location on quiet street;
public secure car parking
Evening meal no
Prices ££££
Rooms 7 double; 3 single; 1
suite; all have telephone, TV,
radio, hairdrier, tea/coffee
kit, trouser press
Facilities roof garden

Smoking restricted
Credit cards AE, MC, V
Children not suitable
Disabled not suitable
Pets no
Closed never
Languages English only
Proprietors Searcy's

London and The South-East

Nutley, S of East Grinstead

Down House

'With nine grandchildren, this isn't likely to look like a hotel,' according to Micky and Gilly Hudson, the sort of easygoing hosts who enjoy having people around. There are prints of horses and dogs on the walls, with antiques and carefully arranged photographs everywhere, but the atmosphere is come-as-you-are. The sitting-room is a place for relaxing, not sitting primly on expensive upholstery. The hosts join guests for dinner at the carved oak table in the open-plan kitchen, 'because we couldn't be in on the conversation if guests sat in the dining-room.'

Bedrooms upstairs are homey, so this is not the place for anyone who wants luxury and designer decorations. Although prices are rather high, guests are happy to pay for the restful setting, with lovely views across to the South Downs. Some use the house as a base for sightseeing, cycling or for walking in Ashdown Forest; others when they go to the opera at Glyndebourne. Mr Hudson once bred horses, so riders are welcome, with their mounts enjoying B&B in the stables.

Nearby Sheffield Park, Wakehurst Place and Nymans gardens.
Directions 9 miles S of East Grinstead. Take A22 S to Nutley. Turn right at post office on Down Street. Get final directions.

Down Street, Nutley, East Sussex TN22 3LG
Tel and Fax (01825) 712328
Location in farmland near village; ample car parking
Evening meal by request
Prices £££
Rooms 3 double; all have radio, tea/coffee kit
Facilities sitting-room, dining-room; garden, stabling for horses
Smoking outdoors only
Credit cards MC, V

Children over 9
Disabled not suitable
Pets by arrangement
Closed Christmas
Languages French
Proprietors Micky and Gilly Hudson

London and The South-East

The Old Railway Station

Former British Airways purser Lou Rapley has transformed a Victorian train station into an unusual bed-and-breakfast. The building dates from 1894 when Lord Egremont, owner of Petworth House, decided that his guests, who included royalty, deserved to arrive at something grander than a small country station. The trains are long gone, so this is now a peaceful spot. Rooms in the former station have a frilly Victorian feel. Breakfast is served in the ticket office, or, in summer, on the platform.

Open since 1996, plans for expansion are now well underway. Mrs. Rapley has acquired two 80 year-old Pullman carriages which stand in their own siding. Furnished like the glamorous Orient Express, they have proper sleeping quarters, bathrooms and even a small sitting-room. A ring at the bell in the morning announces breakfast, served with style on a silver tray. Petworth itself is a stroll away, known for excellent antiques shops as well as Petworth House, one of the National Trust's best-known properties. The pub at the end of the road serves dinner, but reservations are essential on weekends.

Nearby Petworth House, Sussex Downs
Directions on the edge of town. Get directions.

Petworth, West Sussex GU28 0JF	**Credit cards** AE, DC, MC, V
Tel and Fax (01798) 342346	**Children** not suitable
E-mail mlr@old-station.co.uk	**Disabled** not suitable
Location on edge of town; ample car parking	**Pets** no
Evening meal no	**Closed** never
Prices ££-£££	**Languages** English only
Rooms 6 double; all have TV, radio, hairdrier, tea/coffee kit, refrigerator	**Proprietor** Mrs M. Rapley
Facilities sitting-room; garden, station platform	
Smoking outdoors only	

London and The South-East

Rushlake Green, SE of Heathfield

Great Crouch's

A few steps south of the sloping village green is Great Crouch's Farm, now a large family home, with a neatly planted garden and small indoor exercise pool. The real attraction here is the magnificent Sussex barn, now converted into an unusual and delightful place to stay. Under the centuries-old oak beams and vaulted roof stands a wood-burning stove with logs stacked ready for chilly weather. The large room has sofas and armchairs at one end, a large double bed at the other. The pretty, pale blue bathroom is off to one side. Anyone seeking total privacy will find it here, since The Barn is well away from the red-tiled, red brick house. This dates back to around 1720 and has two more bedrooms, though these are only available in summer.

Richard and Ruth Thomas opened to guests in 1995 but chose not to offer dinner at all. That is no problem, since there is a choice of country pubs nearby. The family pets are small Cairns terriers but these are dealt with firmly: at the first signs of canine overexcitement, they are banished to an enclosure.

Nearby Ashdown Forest, Rudyard Kipling home, Sissinghurst.
Directions 5 miles SE of Heathfield. Take B2096 for Battle. Turn right to Rushlake Green. House is south of village green.

Rushlake Green, East Sussex TN21 9QD	**Children** not suitable
Tel (01435) 830145	**Disabled** not suitable
Location on edge of village; ample car parking	**Pets** no
Evening meal no	**Closed** 2 weeks Dec
Prices £££	**Languages** English only
Rooms 3 double; all have TV, radio, tea/coffee kit	**Proprietors** Richard and Ruth Thomas
Facilities dining-room; garden, indoor heated exercise pool	
Smoking outdoors only	
Credit cards MC, V	

London and The South-East

Rye

Little Orchard House

With its cobbled streets and timbered houses, Rye is firmly on the tourist map. Over the centuries, this village near the mouth of the River Rother has been the haunt of sailors, smugglers and the American novelist Henry James. On a quiet lane off the busy main street, a gate leads to a courtyard and Little Orchard House. This dates from about 1720, which 'makes it modern in Rye,' according to owner Sara Brinkhurst, who left the advertising rat race in London and opened in 1990.

One bedroom is dedicated to Prime Minister Lloyd George, who 'is supposed to have stayed here'. The largest room, it has a masculine feel with its original Georgian panelling and marble fireplace. The Garden Room, which looks out on to a magnolia tree, has an oak four-poster made by Sara's partner Robert, who is a furniture maker. As she points out, 'modern four-posters are, thankfully, longer and wider than most antique versions.' In popular destinations such as Rye, some hosts become complacent; we applaud Sara's constant improvements to decorations and comforts. Book early, particularly in high season.

Nearby Heritage Centre, Lamb House; beaches, golf.
Directions West Street is off the main street in Rye.

West Street, Rye, East Sussex
TN31 7ES
Tel and Fax (01797) 223831
Location in quiet street;
public car parking
Evening meal no
Prices £££
Rooms 3 double; all have TV,
radio, hairdrier, tea/coffee
kit; 2 have small refrigerators
Facilities sitting-room; small
walled garden
Credit cards MC, V
Children no

Pets no
Closed never
Languages English only
Proprietor Sara Brinkhurst

London and The South-East

Winchelsea, W of Rye

Cleveland House

Perched on the cliffs above the English Channel, Winchelsea is one of the prettiest villages in south-east England. Instead of narrow winding lanes, the cottages and white-painted houses stand on a neat grid of streets laid out 700 years ago – England's first example of town planning.

Cleveland House, the home of the Jempsons, dates from the 18thC, and has a breathtaking view to the east, over the walled garden with its unusual obelisk, to the sea. Mrs Jempson is a self-confessed 'serious gardener' and spends hours every week on the lawns, greenhouse and flowers which are at their best in the spring and early summer. Guests can laze away the day outside, taking advantage of the heated swimming-pool.

Despite all the antique furniture, the house itself is very light and uncluttered, with large windows. The two comfortable bedrooms, which adjoin one another, have their own staircase, which makes them ideal for friends going away for a break. Breakfast is taken in the dining-room with its fine 18thC French chestnut table and late-18thC English chairs.

Nearby Rye, Great Dixter, Sissinghurst gardens; golf.
Directions 2 miles W of Rye. In village. Get final directions.

Winchelsea, East Sussex
TN36 4EE
Tel (01797) 226256
Location in peaceful village; ample car parking
Evening meal no
Prices £££
Rooms 2 double; all have TV, radio, hairdrier, tea/coffee kit
Facilities sitting-room, dining-room; garden, heated outdoor swimming-pool
Smoking outdoors only

Credit cards MC, V
Children not suitable
Disabled not suitable
Pets no
Closed never
Languages English only
Proprietor Mrs Sarah Jempson

47
➡ *More on page 145*

The South and Channel Islands

Maidenhead

Beehive Manor

With its modern housing, Cox Green is no longer the sleepy hamlet it once was, but Beehive Manor has all the history anyone could possibly want. 'A little oasis of the 16thC' was our inspector's reaction to this black-and-white, half-timbered house, covered by clematis and wisteria and shut off from the 20thC by high hedges. Two weathered carved heads on old beams guard the front door; one impishly sticking out its tongue, as if to put off visitors. One leaded window bears the date 1560, and most are inset with fragments of stained glass. 'These would have come from a monastery, after King Henry VIII destroyed them and shut them down,' owner Bar Barbour explains.

She and her sister, Sue Lemin, totally restored the house, putting in modern plumbing but leaving sloping floors and creaking stairs. Bedrooms do not have televisions, 'because that would spoil the sense of being in a home'. Expect comfort rather than luxury, and a sociable atmosphere. Twenty minutes from Heathrow Airport and near motorways, this is much-used as the first or last night of a holiday in England.

Nearby Marlow, Henley-on-Thames, Windsor, Oxford.
Directions near exit 8/9 of M4. Difficult to find. Get directions.

Cox Green, Maidenhead, Berkshire SL6 3ET
Tel (01628) 620980
Fax (01628) 621840
Location in quiet residential area; some car parking
Evening meal no
Prices £££
Rooms 3 double; some have radio
Facilities sitting-room, dining-room; garden
Smoking outdoors only
Credit cards MC, V

Children over 12
Disabled not suitable
Pets no
Closed Christmas
Languages French, Spanish
Proprietors Bar Barbour, Sue Lemin

The South and Channel Islands

Monkton Farleigh, E of Bath

Fern Cottage

'What a pity that visitors to nearby Bath and Bradford-on-Avon don't know about Monkton Farleigh.' That was the reaction of one American, who was charmed by this unspoiled stone village that even English guidebooks overlook. It has one shop, a pub, a church dating back to Norman times and a primary school. Named after a Clunic monastery destroyed by King Henry VIII, Monkton Farleigh huddles on a hill, one of the Cotswold chain.

Christopher and Jenny Valentine fell in love with the place back in 1970. She is a trained designer, whose confident use of colour shows in the furnishings of their cottage. It has the low beams, thick walls and huge fireplace that are typical of the 17thC, but the two ovens are unusual. 'The smaller would have been used for bread, so the larger must have had a commercial use, but it's a bit of a mystery.' Two bedrooms are upstairs, a third is over the coach house. Quiet and peaceful, this is the sort of place where guests chat over a glass of wine in the conservatory or in the well-tended garden, with its pond and magnolia. Then they may decide to have dinner together in the pub.

Nearby Bath, Bradford-on-Avon; walking.
Directions 5 miles E of Bath. Get final directions.

Monkton Farleigh, Nr
Bradford-on-Avon, BA15 2QJ
Tel (01225) 859412
Fax (01225) 859018
Location in heart of village; own car parking
Evening meal no
Prices ££
Rooms 3 double; all have TV, radio, hairdrier, tea/coffee kit
Facilities dining-room, conservatory; garden
Smoking outdoors only

Credit cards no
Children over 10
Disabled not suitable
Pets no
Closed never
Languages German
Proprietors Christopher and Jenny Valentine

The South and Channel Islands

Romsey

Spursholt House

There is a long gardening tradition at Spursholt House. It was built by one of Cromwell's commanders, General Fletcher, who was fascinated by plants. Today, the grounds include well-clipped topiary and lawns, flowering trees and a parterre. In addition, many guests are garden-lovers who use this as a base while visiting Mottisfont Abbey, home of the National Trust's collection of old-fashioned roses, Hilliers Arboretum and Longstock Water Gardens.

Although the house dates from the 17thC, it was added on to over the years, with major additions from the 19thC including the elegant sitting-room, where doors open on to the terrace. Anthea Hughes has hosted guests since 1990, but the ambience here remains 'family' rather than 'business'. The house has a pleasingly lived-in feel, with invitations on the mantelpiece, photographs and collectibles. For a 17thC ambience, choose the room panelled in original oak; those who insist on an en suite bathroom should ask for the bedroom at the back, where windows overlook the garden.

Nearby Romsey, Winchester, Salisbury; Broadlands; gardens.
Directions 1 mile NW of Romsey. Get directions.

Salisbury Road, Romsey
SO51 6DJ
Tel (01794) 512229
Location in countryside; ample car parking
Evening meal no
Prices ££
Rooms 3 double; all have tea/coffee kit
Facilities sitting-room, dining-room; garden, croquet
Smoking outdoors only
Credit cards no
Children welcome

Disabled not suitable
Pets yes
Closed Christmas
Languages French
Proprietor Anthea Hughes

The South and Channel Islands

Sherfield English, W of Romsey

Wellow Mead

Wellow Mead is one of the most romantic places to stay we have seen anywhere. People come here to celebrate engagements, for honeymoons and to get away from everyday family life. Tucked deep in the countryside, a long drive curves around to an old orchard, a garden overflowing with flowers and Julia Montgomery's 17thC thatched cottage.

Guests may choose from three comfortable and totally separate 'suites'. One, a wing of the house, has its own inglenook fireplace and ancient oak staircase. Two more are in converted buildings once used for storing grain and onions. Both have a stylishly rustic look. In summer, guests may use the barbecue and eat under a striped tent. From May to October, the swimming-pool in the plant-filled conservatory is available for 'candlelit swims'. Although families sometimes book the Onion Store, Wellow Mead is designed as a retreat for couples. It once belonged to the estate of Florence Nightingale's family. The founder of modern nursing is known for her devotion to duty; what would she have thought of this island of romance?

Nearby Romsey, Winchester, Salisbury; Broadlands, gardens.
Directions 4 miles W of Romsey. Get final directions.

Wellow Mead, Sherfield English, Romsey, Hampshire SO51 6DU
Tel (01794) 323227
Location in quiet countryside; ample car parking
Evening meal no
Prices ££££
Rooms 3 suites; all have tea/coffee kit; 1 has a refrigerator
Facilities indoor swimming-pool; garden
Smoking outdoors only

Credit cards no
Children welcome
Disabled not suitable
Pets no
Closed by arrangement in winter
Languages French
Proprietor Julia Montgomery

The South and Channel Islands

Sutton Veny, SE of Warminster

The Old House

Located on the edge of the West Wiltshire Downs, the Old House makes a first-class base for sightseeing. 'There are 14 days' worth of things to do,' claims Bridget Thompson, 'from the ancient stone circles of Avebury to the gardens of Stourhead'. There is even a ruined church just down the road that is 'perfect for an evening stroll, though some guests prefer to stay here and play tennis or croquet.' Mrs Thompson is an unflappable hostess who quickly puts visitors at their ease. She also produces first-rate dinners which, according to season, may feature game, vegetables from the garden and trout caught in the River Test by her fly-fisherman husband, Colin.

Built on the site of an ancient coaching inn, the house dates from 1699. Additions over the years have diluted the feel of any particular era, so this is not the 'step back in time' some may be seeking. However, it will suit those who enjoy the ambience of a gracious family home. Bedrooms are comfortable, not deluxe; bathrooms are private but a few steps down the hall.

Nearby Longleat, Stourhead Gardens, Wilton House.

Directions 4 miles SE of Warminster. Take A36, the bypass, for Salisbury. Difficult to find, get directions.

Sutton Veny, Warminster, Wiltshire BA12 7AQ
Tel (01985) 840344; mobile (0831) 200453
Location on hill outside village; ample car parking
Evening meal by request
Prices £££
Rooms 3 double
Facilities sitting-room, dining-room; garden, tennis court, croquet
Smoking restricted
Credit cards MC, V

Children over 6
Disabled not suitable
Pets no
Closed Christmas, New Year
Languages English only
Proprietors Bridget and Colin Thompson

The South and Channel Islands

Upper Clatford, S of Andover

Fishing Cottage

The name of this bed-and-breakfast proclaims the chosen sport of Julie Maffe. She took up fly-fishing in 1992 and fell in love with this cottage because of its idyllic setting on the peaceful River Anton. This is one of the chalk streams that flow into the River Test, known to the fly-fishing fraternity the world over.

The house was built in 1843, but has been completely renovated. Now, behind the traditional façade, the ground floor is open-plan. Large windows look straight on to the terrace garden and water, where ducks swim and the odd kingfisher can be spotted. On fine summer mornings breakfast may be taken outside. Mrs Maffe hails from the United States but offers the classic English breakfast as well as American treats such as waffles or French toast with maple syrup.

The bedrooms are stylish, if rather small, with a charming cosiness. One is in the main house; the thatched 'Bothey', across the lane offers more privacy. Choose between the double or the roomier suite with mini kitchen. Even if you are not an angler, we recommend this for comfort and value for money.

Nearby Stonehenge, Salisbury, Winchester; gardens, fishing.
Directions 1 mile S of Andover. Get directions.

Upper Clatford, Andover, Hampshire SP11 7HB
Tel and Fax (01264) 364214
Location on quiet lane by river; ample car parking
Evening meal by request
Prices ££–£££
Rooms 2 double; 1 suite; 1 with mini refrigerator, 1 with mini kitchen
Facilities sitting-room, dining-room; terrace
Smoking outdoors only
Credit cards no

Children not suitable
Disabled not suitable
Pets no
Closed Christmas, New Year
Languages English only
Proprietor Julie Maffe

The South and Channel Islands

Upper Clatford, S of Andover

Malt Cottage

Just upstream from Fishing Cottage (*see p53*), Malt Cottage makes another fine place to stay in the pretty, undiscovered village of Upper Clatford. The Masons converted the barn, once used by the village brewer, and the adjacent gardener's cottage into a large, family home. Lawns run down to the River Anton, a tributary of the River Test, where a bench on the bank allows guests to relax and admire the beautiful setting. Richard Mason is a garden designer and the grounds of Malt House reflect his skill. His hobby, however, is fly-fishing and he can make arrangements for anglers to fish for salmon and trout on the Anton and Test. These chalk streams are among the most exclusive in the world, so this is an expensive activity.

For those who do not fish, there is plenty to see nearby. As well as Salisbury, Stonehenge and Winchester, there are gardens and country houses. For those who do not want to drive, Patsy Mason offers conducted tours. Two bedrooms at Malt Cottage are large, a third is smaller but all are well-furnished. The Masons do not offer dinner but there are pubs nearby.

Nearby Stonehenge, Salisbury, Winchester; gardens, fishing.
Directions 1 mile S of Andover. Get directions.

Upper Clatford, Andover, Hampshire SP11 7QL	**Smoking** outdoors only
Tel (01264) 323469	**Credit cards** no
Fax (01264) 334100	**Children** welcome
E-mail maltcottage.accommodation	**Disabled** not suitable
Location on riverbank; own car parking	**Pets** no
Evening meal no	**Closed** never
Prices ££–£££	**Languages** English only
Rooms 3 double; all have radio, tea/coffee kit; 2 have TV	**Proprietors** Richard and Patsy Mason
Facilities sitting-room, dining-room; garden	

The South and Channel Islands

Martens House

The River Thames sweeps through London in huge loops, past famous sights such as the Houses of Parliament and the Tower of London. Its higher reaches have a different character. The river that passes Martens House is a quiet waterway, with small boats chugging from lock to lock, and fields on the far bank.

Lis and Richard Butler have lived here since 1994. Among their first guests were crews rowing in the annual international regatta at nearby Henley-on-Thames. Since then, less energetic visitors have made this a base for sightseeing in Windsor and Oxford. We would enjoy spending a peaceful day on the Thames itself, either walking along the Thames Path or with the Butlers' son, Adrian, in the family's motorized antique punt or the *Painted Bucket*, a small, cheerfully-painted old canal boat.

Martens House is a large, well-furnished, turn-of-the-century family home. A favourite of the well-priced rooms is the main bedroom, with views over the lawn to the river.

A delightful setting, and only half an hour's drive from Heathrow Airport.

Nearby Windsor, Oxford; boating, walking.
Directions 5 miles SW of Maidenhead. Get directions.

Willow Lane, Wargrave, Berkshire RG10 8LH
Tel and Fax (0118) 940 3707
Location on the River Thames; ample car parking
Evening meal no
Prices ££
Rooms 3 double; all have tea/coffee kit
Facilities sitting-room, dining-room; garden, boats
Smoking permitted
Credit cards no
Children welcome

Disabled not suitable
Pets yes
Closed Christmas, New Year
Languages French
Proprietors Lis and Richard Butler

The South and Channel Islands

Winsley, SE of Bath

Burghope Manor

'Remember the Sabbath day to keep it holy.' The Latin version of this commandment is carved on the enormous stone fireplace in the manor's Cranmer Room. This small sitting-room is named after Henry VIII's Archbishop, who reputedly stayed here in the 16thC. By then, the house was already several centuries old; it was 'modernized' back in 1270. 'When you sit in the Cranmer Room of an evening, with the fire flickering, the sense of history is overpowering,' according to proprietor John Denning.

He and his wife, Elizabeth, bought the Grade II listed house 25 years ago, renovated it and filled the downstairs with antiques and portraits. Don't expect the same 'olde worlde' atmosphere upstairs; bedrooms are comfortable rather than historic.

All hosts have information on local sights, but the Dennings go further. They have devised 24 different tours, putting in some of the lesser-known stately homes and charming villages. Dinner is a special, candlelit occasion, but it is available only if a group of friends has booked all three bedrooms.

Nearby Bath, Bradford-on-Avon; museums; Westwood Manor.
Directions 6 miles SE of Bath. Take B3108 to Winsley village. Get final directions.

Winsley, Nr Bradford-on-Avon, Wiltshire BA15 2LA
Tel (01225) 723557
Fax (01225) 723113
Location in own grounds on edge of village; ample car parking
Evening meal by request (see above)
Prices ££££
Rooms 3 double plus separate cottage; all have TV
Facilities sitting-room, dining-room; garden

Smoking restricted
Credit cards MC, V
Children over 10
Disabled not suitable
Pets no
Closed Christmas, New Year
Languages French
Proprietors Elizabeth and John Denning

➡ *More on page 149*

The South-West

Bath

Apsley House Hotel

With a history dating back to the Romans and the elegance of Georgian architecture, Bath justifies its position at the top of the most tourists' must-see lists. Since it is equally popular with home-grown visitors, reservations must be made well in advance.

David and Annie Lanz looked all over the country before falling in love with this impressive house, built for the Duke of Wellington in 1830. With nine bedrooms and 'hotel' in the title, some may argue that Apsley House is outside the bed-and-breakfast category. We are happy to include it because breakfast is the only meal served, there is no concierge or porter, and David and Annie Lanz succeed in creating a warm atmosphere. It will suit those who want antiques and comfort but none of the clutter of family life. 'That is just what we want when we have a break from home and children,' David Lanz explains. Although Newbridge Hill is a busy road, all but three of the rooms are at the back, overlooking the garden. This is a lovely spot for relaxing after seeing the sights in Bath.

Nearby Roman Baths, Abbey and museums.
Directions 1 mile W of city in Newbridge Hill. Off A4, Newbridge Road.

---

141 Newbridge Hill, Bath
BA1 3PT
Tel (01225) 336966
Fax (01225) 425462
Location in residential district; own car parking
Evening meal by request
Prices £££–££££
Rooms 9 double; all have telephone, TV, radio, hairdrier, tea/coffee kit
Facilities sitting-room, dining-room; garden
Smoking restricted

Credit cards MC, V
Children over 5
Disabled not suitable
Pets no
Closed Christmas
Languages French
Proprietors David and Annie Lanz

The South-West

Bath

Bloomfield House

Bath is a small, compact city, which makes sightseeing easy. Parking, however, is difficult, but the bed-and-breakfasts we have chosen all have their own spaces for cars. That means guests can walk or take the bus to town, then return by taxi.

On one of the hills to the south side of the city is Bloomfield House. The large 18thC stone mansion looks austere from the outside, but *trompe l'oeil* windows give a clue to the 'restrained flamboyance' within. We could imagine a Regency dandy posing beneath the painted peacock in the semicircular entrance, or a former owner, the turn-of-the-century lord mayor of Bath, welcoming his guests. His bedroom, with its four-poster bed, is a favourite with honeymooners but every bedroom, even the smallest, is deluxe.

In our opinion, staying here would enhance any visit to Bath, though prices are rather high during the peak season. In winter, however, rates become more reasonable, particularly for this kind of luxury.

Nearby Roman Baths, Abbey and museums.
Directions 1 mile S of city in residential district. Bloomfield Road is off A367, Wellsway.

146 Bloomfield Road, Bath BA2 2AS	**Credit cards** MC, V
Tel (01225) 420105	**Children** over 10
Fax (01225) 481958	**Disabled** not suitable
Location on residential street; own car parking	**Pets** no
Evening meal no	**Closed** never
Prices £££–££££	**Languages** Portuguese
Rooms 8 double; all have telephone, TV, hairdrier, tea/coffee kit	**Proprietors** Bridget and Malcolm Cox
Facilities sitting-room, dining-room; garden	
Smoking outdoors only	

The South-West

Meadowland

Don't expect a house with a history dating back to the days when Jane Austen lived in Bath. Meadowland was built in 1920 as a spacious, family home ... which is what it remains today. 'Each of the paintings and drawings on the walls means something to me,' Catherine Andrew explains. Despite living in England for many years, she still has a soft Scottish accent. She makes Scotch pancakes and potato scones for breakfast and puts Black Watch tartan tablecloths in the dining-room 'because I fancied a little bit of Scotland here in the middle of Bath.'

The house is set back from the street in a large garden. All bedrooms have large windows, giving them a bright and airy look. Mrs Andrew has the knack of mixing colours and patterns, which makes a change from the bland, boring furnishings we have seen in other, more commercial, establishments. Overall, this is a relaxing, comfortable place. At the end of a day's hard sightseeing, stepping through the front door would feel almost like coming home.

Nearby Roman Baths, Abbey and museums.

Directions 1 mile S of city in residential district. Bloomfield Park is off A367, Wellsway.

---

36 Bloomfield Park, Bath
BA2 2BX
Tel (01225) 311079
Location in quiet residential street; own car parking
Evening meal no
Prices £££
Rooms 3 double; all have TV, radio, hairdrier, tea/coffee kit
Facilities sitting-room, dining-room; garden
Smoking outdoors only
Credit cards MC, V

Children over 5
Disabled not suitable
Pets no
Closed never
Languages English only
Proprietor Catherine Andrew

The South-West

Chittlehamholt, SE of Barnstaple

Mole Cottage

Want to learn to throw a pot? Mark and Pauline Donaldson offer bed-and-breakfast with a difference in their 17thC thatched cottage deep in the idyllic Mole Valley. Mark is a member of the League of Professional Craftsmen and his 'architectural ceramics', such as chimney pots and dragon finials, are shipped all over the world. He also has long experience of teaching and can initiate anyone into the techniques of working with clay.

Those who prefer to keep their hands clean visit Rosemoor Garden, a stately home such as Arlington Court, or the Dartington crystal factory. Anglers can cast for salmon or trout in the Mole River. In the house, bedrooms are simple but pretty, with bare boards, lacy curtains and potted plants. The road is just outside, so the rural peace may be broken occasionally by a passing car. In the summer, teas are served in the riverside garden, but in the evening, this is just for guests. The Donaldsons are outgoing and fun to be with. Add in the attractive prices and this is a spot well worth considering.

Nearby Rosemoor Garden, Exmoor, coast; fishing.
Directions 15 miles SE of Barnstaple. Take A361 E to South Molton, then B3226. Get directions.

Watertown, Chittlehamholt, Devon EX37 9HF
Tel and Fax (01769) 540471;
E-mail relax@moley.uk.com
Location on valley road; own car parking
Evening meal by request
Prices ££
Rooms 2 double; 1 single; all have TV, hairdrier, tea/coffee kit
Facilities sitting-room, dining-room; riverside garden, fishing

Smoking outdoors only
Credit cards no
Children welcome
Disabled not suitable
Pets no
Closed Christmas
Languages Polish, some French
Proprietors Mark and Pauline Donaldson

The South-West

Chudleigh, S of Exeter

Oakfield

Chudleigh is one of those in-between places: in between the resort beaches and Dartmoor, in between Exeter and Dartmouth. However, the 1,000-year-old wool town has found a new lease of life as a colony for craft workers. The Johnson-Kings have their own small business, making high-quality signs. Their home is huge, set on a hillside, with a massive fallen tree resting on the lawn 'like a dinosaur' according to children who were playing on it when our inspector arrived. A heated outdoor pool behind the house is big enough for swimming lengths.

'To me, it is a pleasure when people have a wonderful time,' is Mrs Johnson-King's straightforward philosophy. Set in 20 acres of gardens, paddocks and orchards, the 1840 house is luxurious-ly furnished but with enough photos of happy children to emphasize that this is a family home. All the bedrooms are pret-ty, but the Chinese Room stands out with its black bed covers and peach tones. For this quality, prices are extremely attractive; several restaurants are within walking distance.

Nearby Dartmoor National Park, Torbay; golf, fishing, riding.

Directions 10 miles S of Exeter. Take A38 for Plymouth. Turn off for Chudleigh. House on right before middle of town.

Chudleigh, Devon
TQ13 0DD
Tel (01626) 852194
Location on hillside on edge of town; ample car parking
Evening meal no
Prices ££
Rooms 4 double; all have TV, radio, hairdrier, tea/coffee kit
Facilities sitting-room, dining-room, billiards room; garden, heated outdoor swimming-pool

Smoking outdoors only
Credit cards no
Children over 12
Disabled not suitable
Pets no
Closed end Oct to before Easter
Languages English only
Proprietors Patricia and Peter Johnson-King

The South-West

Crackington Haven, S of Bude

Manor Farm

Crackington Haven is just a cleft in the North Cornwall coastline, with a tiny cove and beach guarded by enormous, wild cliffs. Rather than sunbathing, this is a place for windswept walks that blow the mental cobwebs away.

Like so many places with 'farm' in the name, Manor Farm is no longer an agricultural business. Metal gates and a gravel driveway lead to the 11thC granite manor house set in geometrically-mown lawns that look 'like a park, with every blade of grass in place,' according to one awed visitor. Inside, the house is equally immaculate, full of antiques and pot-pourri. Muriel Knight's meals are both memorable and a bargain: shell-fish mousse, pheasant casserole, individual desserts, cheeses and Belgian chocolates with coffee. 'Almost too much,' for one lady who was reduced to asking for fruit for breakfast.

Some may find the schedule a little rigid. Drinks, dinner and breakfast are served communally, at set times, which suits older folk but perhaps not those seeking romantic relaxation. Enclosed by meadows, Manor Farm is a mile from the beach.
Nearby cliff walks, beaches, open countryside; golf, fishing.
Directions 7 miles S of Bude. Take A39. Get final directions.

Crackington Haven, North Cornwall EX23 0JW
Tel (01840) 230304
Location in secluded grounds; ample car parking
Evening meal by request
Prices £££
Rooms 4 double; all have telephone, TV, radio, hairdrier, tea/coffee kit
Facilities sitting-room, dining-room, snooker room; garden
Smoking outdoors only
Credit cards no

Children not suitable
Disabled not suitable
Pets no
Closed Christmas
Languages English only
Proprietors Muriel and Paul Knight

The South-West

Trevigue

We hardly know where to begin to describe this farmhouse, perched on top of Cornwall's highest cliffs, with truly spectacular ocean views. The Crockers are passionate about their 500 acres, which have been farmed for 1,000 years and are mentioned in the Domesday Book. Their care for the land has brought the return of rare wildlife, from butterflies to otters. Their 16thC farmhouse with its cobbled courtyard is equally well maintained: expect antiques and a medieval atmosphere. From the slate-floored hall, the oak staircase leads to bedrooms which are snug but have modern comforts. Samphire House, a separate, modern villa nearby, has two more bedrooms, but guests staying here join others in the main house for meals.

Mrs Crocker's dinners, served at separate tables, are what bring visitors back, time and again. As a farmer's wife she likes to cook for hearty appetites, with specialities such as game pie. We recommend Trevigue as a fine example of a tasteful conversion, where the owners take professional care of their guests and offer traditional hospitality.

Nearby cliff walks, beaches, open countryside; golf, fishing.
Directions 7 miles S of Bude. Take A39. Get final directions.

Crackington Haven, North Cornwall, EX23 0LQ
Tel and Fax (01840) 230418
Location on cliff top; ample car parking
Evening meal by request
Prices ££
Rooms 5 double; all have TV, tea/coffee kit
Facilities sitting-room, dining-room; garden, heated outdoor swimming-pool (by arrangement)
Smoking restricted

Credit cards no
Children over 12
Disabled not suitable
Pets no
Closed Christmas
Languages English only
Proprietor Janet Crocker

The South-West

Dartmouth

Ford House

Dartmouth is a dapper naval town, with well-clipped gardens and plenty of antiques shops, full of nautical knick-knacks. Ford House has a fine position on a hillside, with views over the houses and River Dart estuary. Those who enjoy walking will be able to leave their cars here and not have the problem of finding a parking space in the town.

Richard Turner is a tall, affable Australian who spends eight months of the year in Dartmouth and four months in Melbourne, 'tasting the wines'. He also has firm views on how to run a luxury bed-and-breakfast. For a start, breakfast is served right through until noon. The four-course dinners are praised, ranging from warm quail with a mesclun salad to fresh local fish, enterprising desserts and English cheeses. For groups of friends, Richard offers Dinner Party Weekends, which include lunch at the famous Carved Angel restaurant in town. The bedrooms in this 1820s house are decorated boldly, with plenty of colour and pattern. Beds are angled to make the most of the views. 'Expensive? Yes, but worth every penny,' one guest told us.

Nearby River Dart, boat trips, steam train; fishing, walking.
Directions Victoria Road is in Victoria Heights, W of harbour.

---

44 Victoria Road, Dartmouth, Devon TQ6 9DX
Tel and Fax (01803) 834047
Location on quiet road, above town; ample car parking
Evening meal by request
Prices ££££
Rooms 3 double; all have telephone, TV, radio, hairdrier, tea/coffee kit, refrigerators
Facilities sitting-room, dining-room; small walled garden
Smoking permitted

Credit cards AE, MC, V
Children welcome
Disabled not suitable
Pets yes
Closed Nov to Feb
Languages English only
Proprietor Richard Turner

The South-West

Dittisham, W of Dartmouth

The White House

Deep in Devon's holiday country, Dittisham stands on the west bank of the River Dart which broadens into a wide estuary as it nears Dartmouth and the sea. Once known for cider and plums, this attractive village, with thatched and stone-built cottages, is now popular with sailors.

In 1998, Jill and Hugh Treseder expanded their 18thC home, with its pillared entrance. Now their two front rooms have delightful views over the water; the twin-bedded room is at the rear. More suited to couples than families, visitors come to enjoy the simple things in life. In spring, many head for the peaceful country lanes and footpaths. In summer, the coastal paths offer dramatic views of the sea.

Historic towns such as Dartmouth and Totnes are nearby. "Many guests arrive by car, but after a couple of days they park it and spend the rest of their holiday on foot." The sailing school is a few steps away, as are two popular pubs. The Ferry Boat Inn is down on the water, while the Red Lion, with a restaurant for evening meals, also has views of the river .

Nearby River Dart, Dartmouth, Totnes, Dartmoor.
Directions above town. Get final directions.

Manor Street, Dittisham, Devon TQ6 0EX
Tel and Fax (01803) 722355
E-mail Treseder@compuserve.com
Location above the town; ample car parking
Evening meal no
Prices £££
Rooms 3 double; all have TV, hairdrier, tea/coffee kit
Facilities sitting-room; terrace, garden
Smoking outdoors only
Credit cards no

Children not suitable
Disabled not suitable
Pets no
Closed Christmas
Languages English only
Proprietors Hugh and Jill Treseder

The South-West

Pennard Hill Farm

Every now and then we find a place that is truly extraordinary, and this is it: a converted Victorian farmhouse complex set on a hilltop and decorated with the panache of a top interior designer. 'I come from a family of artists,' is the matter-of-fact explanation of owner Phoebe Judah. Her choice of colours is sure and her taste eclectic, ranging from antique Italian and French beds to carved stone heads of Neptune from a seaside pier.

Her theory is simple: 'I treat people as my house guests.' There is no enforced sociability, however, since there are only three 'suites'. Those staying in the main house have a large sitting-room as well as two stylish bedrooms upstairs. Across the courtyard, the stable block is totally private. Mrs Judah stocks up the kitchen so guests can make breakfast whenever they please. Next door is an indoor swimming-pool, with stunning views through a Gothic-arched window across to the Mendip Hills. Prices here are among the highest in this book, but regulars are happy to pay for the luxury and exclusivity.

Nearby Glastonbury, Wells, Wookey Hole, vineyard.
Directions 5 miles SW of Shepton Mallet off A37. Very difficult to find. Get directions.

Stickleball Hill, East Pennard, Shepton Mallet, Somerset BA4 6UG
Tel (01749) 890221
Fax (01749) 890665
Location in meadows on crest of hill; ample car parking
Evening meal by request
Prices ££££
Rooms 3 suites; both have TV, radio, hairdrier; 1 has a kitchen
Facilities sitting-room, dining-room; garden, indoor heated swimming-pool
Smoking permitted
Credit cards no
Children not suitable
Disabled not suitable
Pets by arrangement
Closed never
Languages English only
Proprietor Phoebe Judah

The South-West

Elmscott, SW of Bideford

Docton Mill

The northwest coast of Devon is wild and rough, yet just inland lie tiny, tranquil valleys. One of these is Spekes Valley, where Docton Mill looks almost overgrown by lush greenery. Martin and Eva Bourcier moved here in 1993 to fulfil their dream of living in a watermill. This one dates from Saxon times and produced flour for 1,100 years until it finally closed in 1910.

Keen gardeners might know the place from television programmes and books, which have featured its unusual 'bog garden'. During the day, the grounds are open to the public, but at 6 pm, the atmosphere becomes private. There are only two bedrooms and both show the Bourciers' attention to detail, with high-quality beds and fine linens. Urban intrusions such as telephones and televisions are confined to other parts of the house. These hosts aim to cater for every need, so a cup of tea is 'when you want it' and breakfast is 'anytime you like'. Prices may look a bit high, but few places can match the combination of comfort and seclusion. This is a welcome retreat from everyday life.

Nearby Rosemoor and Marwood Hill gardens, Clovelly, coast.

Directions 12 miles SW of Bideford. Take A39 for Bude, then B3248 to Hartland. Get final directions.

Lymebridge, Elmscott, Nr Hartland, Devon EX39 6EA
Tel and Fax (01237) 441369
Location in hidden valley; ample car parking
Evening meal by request
Prices ££££
Rooms 2 double
Facilities sitting-room, dining-room; terrace, garden
Smoking outdoors only
Credit cards MC, V
Children over 14
Disabled not suitable

Pets no
Closed Christmas, New Year
Languages Polish, some French
Proprietors Martin and Eva Bourcier

The South-West

Glastonbury

Number Three

Number Three couldn't be easier to find, since it is right on Glastonbury's main street. For many years, it was a restaurant with rooms but, in 1997, when Pat and Trevor Redmond phoned to reserve a table for their wedding anniversary, they discovered the place was for sale. So they bought it. 'Coming here was a natural progression,' they told us. After living in Africa they had settled in the Somerset countryside but fancied living in a town. They are not restaurateurs, so breakfast is the only meal offered. It is taken in the main house, but the four comfortable rooms are in the modern house just behind. The element of privacy appeals to those who prefer to avoid the trappings of someone else's family life. A bonus is the large garden, which backs on to the grounds of the famous abbey. This religious house was a powerful institution in the Middle Ages, but pilgrims had been travelling to Glastonbury for centuries. King Arthur's grave is said to be here, while the Holy Grail is supposedly buried on the nearby Tor. Today, the town is known for its pop music festival and its community devoted to alternative lifestyles.

Nearby Mendip Hills, Wells Cathedral, Cheddar Gorge.

Directions Magdalene Street is Glastonbury's main street.

3 Magdalene Street,
Glastonbury, Somerset
BA6 9EW
Tel (01458) 832129
Fax (01458) 843227
Location on main street; own car parking
Evening meal no
Prices ££££
Rooms 4 double; all have telephone, TV, radio, tea/coffee kit
Facilities dining-room; garden, terrace

Smoking outdoors only
Credit cards AE, MC, V
Children welcome
Disabled not suitable
Pets no
Closed Dec to Mar
Languages English only
Proprietors Pat and Trevor Redmond

The South-West

Marston Bigot, SW of Frome

The Old Rectory

In rolling farmland, just a few miles away from Frome, is the hamlet of Marston Bigot, with a small church and large vicarage. The Old Rectory was built in 1835 by the Earl of Cork. He must have been a man of style, since he commissioned an Italianate mansion, with arches, balconies and even a central tower.

We think he would be pleased with the restoration carried out by Christine and Alan Lown. She is a professional designer and chose antiques and furnishings to reflect the age of the house. Choosing between the three bedrooms is difficult. The glamorous Victorian Room comes with a huge four-poster bed and a bathroom big enough for a crowd. The smaller French Room is more feminine, while the Deco Room is pure 1930s nostalgia. No doubt such frivolity would have shocked the vicars who used to live here. So would the luxury and the leisurely four-course dinners. This is a get-away-from-it-all kind of place, so it would be a pity to stay here only one night. Save this for an occasion and then book in with friends.

Nearby Longleat House, Nunney Castle, Chalcot House.
Directions 3 miles SW of Frome. Take A361 for Shepton Mallet. Get final directions.

Marston Bigot, Nr Frome, Somerset BA11 5DA
Tel (01373) 836265
Location surrounded by meadows; ample car parking
Evening meal by request
Prices ££££
Rooms 3 double; all have tea/coffee kit
Facilities sitting-room, dining-room, conservatory; garden, terrace
Smoking restricted
Credit cards MC, V

Children not suitable
Disabled not suitable
Pets no
Closed never
Languages English only
Proprietors Christine and Alan Lown

The South-West

Monkshill

Monkton Combe is just outside Bath, but it is no city suburb. The tiny hamlet of stone buildings lies at the bottom of a narrow valley, or 'combe', through which run the River Avon and the Kennet and Avon Canal. High on a hill, with a panoramic view over the vale, stands Monkshill. 'We bought the house for this view,' Michael and Catherine Westlake told us. That was in 1981. Since then, they have turned the huge garden into a showcase, with terraced lawns and flowering shrubs, a rockery and fountain, plus decorative trees. In 1997, they added an orangery to the side of the house, where guests can enjoy breakfast on summer mornings.

'My guests are my family,' Catherine explains. Not all families have bedrooms as comfortable as these, with expensive fabrics and colour schemes of turquoise, apricot or yellow and blue. First-time guests think of this as a base for exploring Bath and Bradford-on-Avon; regulars return to relax and spend time walking or cycling in the valley, or perhaps renting a boat to chug along the Kennet and Avon Canal.

Nearby Bath, Bradford-on-Avon; cycling, boating on canal.
Directions 4.5 miles SE of Bath. Get final directions.

Shaft Road, Monkton Combe, Bath BA2 7HL
Tel and Fax (01225) 833028
Location in countryside; ample car parking
Evening meal no
Prices ££££
Rooms 3 double; all have TV, hairdrier, tea/coffee kit
Facilities sitting-room, dining-room; garden, croquet
Smoking outdoors only
Credit cards AE, MC, V
Children welcome

Disabled not suitable
Pets by arrangement
Closed Christmas, New Year
Languages Greek
Proprietors Catherine and Michael Westlake

The South-West

Polperro, W of Plymouth

Landaviddy Manor

Polperro is a well-known, picturesque Cornish fishing village, where white and pastel houses cling, limpet-like to the steep hills around the harbour. Although the narrow streets are free of cars, they are clogged with tourists in high season. Landaviddy Manor appeals to us since it is just outside Polperro, cocooned in its own grounds but close to the glorious cliff walks and raging waves that are typical of the Cornish coast. Most guests come to fish, paint and hike rather than to lie on the beach.

Meryl and Eric Rowe have owned the 200-year-old stone mansion since 1994. The seven bedrooms are large, with space for four-poster beds and even a couple of armchairs, 'because guests like to relax in the privacy of their own room with a book'. Meryl, who is Welsh, does not offer dinner but cooks a traditional English breakfast on her Aga, happy to accommodate all tastes. 'I have served Italians, Moslems and vegans. No problem at all.' For some, the overall effect is rather folksy, but the warmth of the welcome and the comfort are genuine.

Nearby Trelissick Gardens, Cotehele, Lanhydrock; fishing.
Directions 28 miles W of Plymouth. Take A387. Awkward single-track lane to house. Get final directions.

Landaviddy Lane, Polperro, Cornwall PL13 2RT
Tel (01503) 272210
Location west of village, on narrow lane; ample car parking
Evening meal no
Prices ££–£££ (minimum 2 nights June to Sep)
Rooms 6 double; 1 suite; all have TV, hairdrier, tea/coffee kit, alarm clocks
Facilities sitting-room, dining-room; garden

Smoking outdoors only
Credit cards MC, V
Children over 14
Disabled not suitable
Pets no
Closed Nov to Feb
Languages English only
Proprietors Eric and Meryl Rowe

The South-West

Polperro, W of Plymouth

Trenderway Farm

This makes another fine place to stay, away from the popular sea-side village of Polperro. The drive alone is delightful, following winding lanes to a shallow ford, and on to the Tuckett family's 500-year-old farmhouse. Although the Tucketts raise beef, none of the stone buildings in the courtyard houses animals, so there is no mud to worry city-dwellers.

Lynne Tuckett has a fine eye for decorating. The two bed-rooms in the main house are feminine, with plenty of frilly white and pastel fabrics. As Trenderway Farm has expanded, so the decoration has become more flamboyant. The two rooms in a converted barn are not only more private, they have bolder colours, uplighters and modern four-poster beds. The spacious bathrooms, however, have traditional Victorian tubs.

In the conservatory, Lynne offers a traditional four-course breakfast or a lighter, continental version. The only drawback is that she does not prepare dinner, but the local 16thC pub is highly rated for both food and atmosphere.

Nearby Talland Bay, Trelissick Gardens; golf, horse riding.
Directions 28 miles W of Plymouth. Take A387. House is between Pelynt and Polperro, get final directions.

Pelynt, Nr Polperro, Cornwall
PL13 2LY
Tel (01503) 272214
Fax (01503) 272991
Location head of a peaceful valley; ample car parking
Evening meal no
Prices ££–£££
Rooms 4 double; all have TV, hairdrier, tea/coffee kit
Facilities sitting-room, conservatory; garden
Smoking outdoors only
Credit cards no

Children not suitable
Disabled not suitable
Pets no
Closed Christmas and New Year
Languages English only
Proprietors Lynne and Anthony Tuckett

The South-West

St Blazey, E of St Austell

Nanscawen House

Our inspector was not the first visitor to be bowled over by the quality of this comfortable home, set in 5 acres in one of the prettiest parts of Cornwall. A string of awards and commendations have recognized that Keith Martin's house is a special place to stay. The report summed it up: 'ten out of ten'.

Hidden away up a long, narrow drive lined with wild flowers, Nanscawen House has panoramic views over the countryside. Wisteria crawls along the stone walls, handsome cedars stand on the lawn and the flower beds burst with colourful shrubs. Don't expect a cosy cottage stuffed with antiques: the interior here is spacious, with everything in immaculate order and stylish modern furniture. Bedrooms are so large that 'even the double beds look dwarfed, while bathrooms have a touch of Hollywood with their glamorous spa baths.'

No wonder an American family who took over the whole house for a week in the spring of 1997 reported that 'this was better than any hotel where we have ever stayed.'

Nearby beaches, Lanhydrock House; golf, riding, walking.
Directions 4 miles E of St Austell. Take A390 to St Blazey. Prideaux Road is on left.

Prideaux Road, St Blazey, Nr Par, Cornwall PL24 2SR
Tel and Fax (01726)814488
E-mail
keithmartin@tesco.net
Location on quiet residential street; ample car parking
Evening meal no
Prices ££££
Rooms 3 double; all have telephone, TV, hairdrier, tea/coffee kit
Facilities sitting-room, conservatory; garden, heated outdoor swimming-pool, whirlpool
Smoking outdoors only
Credit cards MC, V
Children over 12
Disabled not suitable
Pets no
Closed never
Languages English only
Proprietor Keith Martin

The South-West

St Hilary, E of Penzance

Ennys

Hidden away up a country lane, yet only a few minutes' drive from the popular tourist destination of St. Michael's Mount, this 17thC house is clad in creeper and overlooks lawns and a garden. Gill Charlton, who took over the successful business in 1998, is a well-known travel writer. Having seen many bed and breakfasts, she knew exactly what she wanted and was determined to maintain the relaxed atmosphere. Although evening meals are no longer offered, guests who arrive in the afternoon are welcomed with a Cornish cream tea and Gill's home-baked cakes; on subsequent days, they are free to help themselves to the spread laid out in the large kitchen. There are three pretty, traditionally-decorated bedrooms in the main house; two more modern rooms in the converted farm buildings are ideal for families.

There is plenty to do and see nearby, and at the end of the day, the grass tennis court and swimming-pool are available during the summer months. The choice of the name Ennys is appropriate. This Celtic word means isolated farmhouse or oasis. Ennys has something of both.

Nearby St Michael's Mount, Trengwainton Garden, St Ives.
Directions 5 miles E of Penzance. Get final directions.

St Hilary, Penzance, Cornwall TR20 9BZ
Tel (01736) 740262
Fax (01736) 740055
E-mail ennys@zetnet.co.uk
Location in deep countryside; ample car parking
Evening meal by request
Prices £££
Rooms 5 double; all have TV, hairdrier, tea/coffee kit
Facilities sitting-room, dining-room; garden, heated outdoor swimming-pool, grass tennis court
Smoking restricted
Credit cards MC, V
Children welcome
Disabled not suitable
Pets no
Closed Christmas
Languages French, some Spanish
Proprietor Gill Charlton

The South-West

Shaldon, S of Exeter

Fonthill

The first thing we noticed about Fonthill was its unusual free-standing clock tower outside the front door. Since it only strikes at 12 noon and 6 pm, the peace is rarely broken high on this hill-side. We were equally impressed by the 25 acres of grounds, including a grand yew-lined avenue leading to a Greek-style temple whose baptismal font gives the place its name.

The cream Georgian mansion has been the Graeme family home for 130 years and is very much from the old school of bed-and-breakfasts. When the children grew up and left home, their rooms in the West Wing were turned over for the exclusive use of guests, who have their own entrance up wisteria-covered stairs. Compared with the grandeur of the house, the interior is rather dull. The somewhat Spartan breakfast-cum-television room could do with some more pictures, though views of the lawns are lovely. The large guest sitting-room, however, has attractive French windows leading into the garden. Jenny Graeme does not serve dinner, but there are five pubs in the colour-washed village of Shaldon, a five-minute walk away. Useful for an informal break.

Nearby Shaldon village, Dartmoor National Park; golf.
Directions 16 miles S of Exeter. Get final directions.

Torquay Road, Shaldon,
Teignmouth, Devon
TQ14 OAX
Tel and Fax (01626) 872344
E-mail swanphoto2@aol.com
Location on edge of pretty
village; ample car parking
Evening meal no
Prices ££
Rooms 3 double; all have
tea/coffee kit
Facilities sitting-room, dining-room; garden, tennis court
Smoking outdoors only

Credit cards no
Children not suitable
Disabled not suitable
Pets no
Closed Dec to mid-Marz
Languages English only
Proprietors Jenny and
Anthony Graeme

The South-West

The Lynch Country House

Somerton is all too often overlooked by visitors to Somerset. Yet this was once a royal town in the ancient kingdom of Wessex and boasts a photogenic and medieval-looking market square. On the outskirts stands the Lynch Country House in a mature garden, complete with lake and black swans. Formerly a restaurant with rooms, it is now a bed-and-breakfast. Some of the previous formality persists, which suits those who dislike the clutter of family photographs and memorabilia. Similarly, separate tables in the high-ceilinged dining-room allow privacy at breakfast time.

The house has the generous proportions of the early 1800s, plus a 'sun bonnet' at the top. From this cupola, the 360-degree panorama includes the 15thC church tower and the surrounding countryside. Bedrooms vary. The spacious Goldington has an 18thC four-poster bed but we would be just as happy in one of the smaller, less expensive rooms up under the eaves. The bathroom for one of these is just a few steps away, across the landing. Host Roy Copeland is low-key but welcoming; Lottie, his standard poodle, is friendly, if a little overeager.

Nearby Glastonbury, Muchelney Abbey, Castle Cary.
Directions 6 miles S of Glastonbury. Get directions.

4 Behind Berry, Somerton, Somerset TA11 7 PD	**Credit cards** AE, MC, V
Tel (01458) 272316	**Children** not suitable
Fax (01458) 272590	**Disabled** not suitable
Location in own grounds with lake; ample car parking	**Pets** no
Evening meal no	**Closed** Christmas
Prices ££–££££	**Languages** English only
Rooms 5 double; all have telephone, TV, radio, hairdrier	**Proprietor** Roy Copeland
Facilities sitting/dining-room; garden, lake	
Smoking outdoors only	

The South-West

Teignmouth, S of Exeter

Thomas Luny House

'Who was Thomas Luny?' John and Alison Allan are well-used to explaining that he was a naval artist during the time of Admiral Lord Nelson, hero of the Battle of Trafalgar (1805). According to the date over the archway entrance, the house was built in 1792, handily placed just a few steps from the quay in the old quarter of the small port of Teignmouth.

The interior is distinctly elegant and far more comfortable than a run-of-the-mill seaside bed-and-breakfast. Paintwork is fresh, and furniture newly covered, while the garden looks immaculate, with perfect arum lilies and impeccably trained roses. Ladies looking for lace and frills may be disappointed but we liked the restrained decoration, particularly the masculine-looking Luny Room. Here, the appropriately nautical flavour is emphasized by leather armchairs and a massive sea chest.

Prices here are high but so, too, is the quality and the Allans work hard to provide a relaxing stay. To our mind, tea brought to the bedroom in the morning, with a newspaper, is the perfect way to start the day. Dinner is informal, served at one big table.
Nearby Teignmouth, Dartmoor; golf, water sports.
Directions 16 miles S of Exeter. In the old part of Teignmouth.

Teign Street, Teignmouth,
Devon TQ14 8EG
Tel (01626) 772976
Location in quiet street; own
car parking
Evening meal by request
Prices ££££
Rooms 4 double; all have
telephone, TV, radio,
hairdrier
Facilities sitting-room, dining-
room; small walled garden
Smoking restricted
Credit cards no

Children over 12
Disabled not suitable
Pets no
Closed two weeks Dec, Jan
Languages French
Proprietors John and Alison
Allan

The South-West

Trenale, S of Bude

Trebrea Lodge

John Charlick and Sean Devlin have taken bed-and-breakfast to its highest plateau. Some may say that this is a small country hotel or a restaurant with rooms. Instead of arguing about the category, we prefer to enjoy the first-class food and attentive service in sophisticated surroundings. Since the manor house is long and narrow, all seven bedrooms face west to the sea, "so we found it hard to drag ourselves away from the sunset to go down to dinner," one guest lamented.

The wood-panelled dining-room is open to non-residents, so be sure to book for the four-course set dinner. On our visit, the menu offered French onion tart with cucumber salsa, baked salmon fillet, strawberry pavlova and British cheeses. Candles and crisp linen add to the occasion. The snug, with its honesty bar, also admits that rare breed, the smoker. Such elegance deserves proper attire, so T-shirts and shorts are out of place in an atmosphere that is 'ever so slightly stuffy, and therefore ideal for couples who want to retain their own privacy,' according to a duo who wanted to do just that.

Nearby Tintagel, Bodmin Moor, Jamaica Inn; golf, walking.
Directions 14 miles S of Bude. Take A39. Get final directions.

Trenale, Tintagel, Cornwall PL34 0HR	**Credit cards** AE, MC, V
Tel (01840) 770410	**Children** not suitable
Fax (01840) 770092	**Disabled** not suitable
Location set in countryside; ample car parking	**Pets** yes
	Closed Jan, early Feb
Evening meal by request	**Languages** English only
Prices ££££	**Proprietors** John Charlick and Sean Devlin
Rooms 7 double; all have telephone, TV, hairdrier, tea/coffee kit	
Facilities 2 sitting-rooms, dining-room; garden	
Smoking restricted	

The South-West

Wells

Beryl

Reactions vary to this Victorian Gothic mansion, which stands on a hill overlooking the city of Wells. The formal atmosphere appeals to some; others find it a little impersonal. Since 1982, when the Nowells first opened to guests, they have expanded and now have eight rooms for guests. The largest is the spacious Butterfly, with a view towards Glastonbury and the sort of gilt-and-marble bathroom found in five-star hotels. Furnishings throughout are expensive, but some combinations are more successful than others. Our favourite is Spring, in sunny yellow and soft grey, with a four-poster bed and an outlook over the impressive garden and swimming-pool to the cathedral below.

The Nowell dinners have been praised, with vegetables from the garden and Holly's speciality, 'Beryl bread-and-butter pudding' for dessert. Her husband, Eddie, runs an antiques business, which accounts for the grandfather clocks and vases, the china, prints and *objets d'art* throughout the house. With prices that are top of the range, this is a special-occasion place. Don't expect a relaxed, home from home ambience.

Nearby Wells Cathedral, Cheddar Gorge, Wookey Hole.
Directions on eastern outskirts of Wells, off B3139.

Hawkers Lane, Wells, Somerset BA5 3JP
Tel (01749) 678738
Fax (01749) 670508
Location in extensive grounds overlooking Wells; ample car parking
Evening meal by request
Prices £££–££££
Rooms 8 double; all have telephone, TV, radio, hairdrier, tea/coffee kit
Facilities sitting-room, dining-room, library; garden, outdoor heated swimming-pool
Smoking restricted
Credit cards MC, V
Children very welcome
Disabled access to upstairs rooms via stairlift
Pets yes
Closed Christmas
Languages English only
Proprietor Holly Doone Nowell

 ➡ *More on page 153*

East Anglia and The East Midlands

Greenhill, E of Coalville

Abbots Oak

Abbots Oak is one of the most intriguing houses we have seen anywhere. Legend has it that the abbot of the name died under a nearby oak tree after his monastery was seized by King Henry VIII in the 16thC.

Inside, the staircase is said to be from Nell Gwyn's house in London's Pall Mall. Certainly, the oak looks old enough, heavily carved with figures such as a child, a deer, grapes and leaves. Then there are the stained-glass panels above the stairs, with their coats of arms and hard-to-decipher Latin inscriptions. 'We are not sure exactly how old they are, or why they are there,' is the frank admission of Carolyn White. Her parents, Bill and Audrey, have lived here for 50 years but it was her idea to open to guests in 1994. She is also in charge of the evening meal, four courses of 'interesting home-cooking'.

Don't expect designer decorations; this remains very much the family home. Our favourite room is at the back, overlooking the garden and enormous cedar of Lebanon. There is a full-size billiard table, a croquet lawn and a tennis court.

Nearby Ashby-de-la-Zouch, Snibston Discovery Park.

Directions 2 miles from M1, exit 22. Get final directions.

Greenhill, Nr Coalville, Leicestershire LE67 4UY
Tel and Fax (01530) 832328
Location off country road, in extensive gardens; ample car parking
Evening meal by request
Prices £££
Rooms 3 double; all have TV, hairdrier
Facilities 2 sitting-rooms, dining-room; terrace, garden, tennis court
Smoking restricted

Credit cards no
Children welcome
Disabled not suitable
Pets yes
Closed never
Languages English only
Proprietors Audrey, Bill and Carolyn White

East Anglia and The East Midlands

Higham, N of Colchester

The Bauble

Dedham Vale attracts art lovers from all over the world who want to see the countryside that John Constable made famous in paintings such as *The Haywain* and *Flatford Mill*. Two centuries later, The Bauble looks out on the same bucolic scenery, complete with nightingales serenading in the evening. Nowell and Penny Watkins' house dates back to around 1400 and still has an unusual Elizabethan well in the carefully tended garden. This friendly couple have lived here for some 40 years and their home is filled with antiques and grand arrangements of flowers. Penny is punctilious about detail, so her three well-priced bedrooms have towelling bathrobes, local maps to borrow and up-to-date magazines, not 'old ones passed on'.

The tennis court and outdoor swimming-pool are only available to visitors after 4.30 pm and before 10.30 am, 'otherwise, the family can't get near them'. Although the Watkins do not offer dinner, this is not a drawback. After a glass of sherry, they send guests off to one of several fine restaurants nearby, including The Talbooth, one of the best-known in the country.

Nearby Dedham Vale, Flatford Mill, Sudbury, Lavenham.
Directions 7 miles N of Colchester. Get final directions.

Higham, Colchester, Essex
CO7 6LA
Tel (01206) 337254
Fax (01206) 337263
Location on edge of quiet village; ample car parking
Evening meal by request
Prices ££
Rooms 2 double; 1 single; all have TV, radio, hairdrier, tea/coffee kit
Facilities sitting-room, dining-room; garden, terrace, tennis court, heated outdoor swimming-pool
Smoking outdoors only
Credit cards no
Children over 12
Disabled not suitable
Pets no
Closed never
Languages English only
Proprietors Nowell and Penny Watkins

East Anglia and The East Midlands

Hope, W of Sheffield

Underleigh House

Beware: there are two villages named Hope in the Peak District National Park. This one is in Derbyshire, near the caverns of Castleton and the beginning of the Pennine Way at Edale. The High Peaks have long been known as hiking country, though car-bound visitors can also enjoy the rugged beauty of the moors and softer landscapes of the dales.

Barbara and Tony Singleton ran a successful restaurant in Hope for 20 years, then opted for a change of pace in 1987. Since then, they have welcomed guests to their hillside home above the River Noe. Although there are seven bedrooms, the house has the cosy ambience of a smaller building. Views are of the garden, a kaleidoscope of colour, or across the peaceful valley to Win Hill. Most bed-and-breakfasts offer a set menu for the evening meal. Tony, however, is a professional chef, and provides a choice of five dishes for each of the three courses, served at one large table. From Underleigh, the energetic can follow the Ridge Walk to Castleton or walk over to the Derwent Dams, where the famous movie, *The Dambusters*, was filmed.

Nearby Chatsworth, Bakewell, Eyam; riding, walking, golf.

Directions 15 miles W of Sheffield. Get final directions.

off Edale Road, Hope, Derbyshire S33 6RF
Tel (01433) 621372
Fax (01433) 621324
Location above peaceful valley; ample car parking
Evening meal by request
Prices £££
Rooms 7 double; all have telephone, TV, radio, hairdrier, tea/coffee kit
Facilities sitting-room, dining-room; terrace, garden
Smoking restricted

Credit cards MC, V
Children over 12
Disabled not suitable
Pets no
Closed never
Languages English only
Proprietors Tony and Barbara Singleton

East Anglia and The East Midlands

Littlebury Green, W of Saffron Walden

Elmdon Lee

This part of the county of Essex is peaceful and pretty, with trimmed hawthorn hedges bordering tiny lanes, thatched village pubs, and white rails guarding duck ponds. Surprisingly, it is only 25 miles north of London.

Elmdon Lee stands on a rise overlooking undulating farmland, at the end of Littlebury Green, a prosperous dormitory hamlet of expensive cottages and grander houses. Diana Duke is a warm, approachable hostess who, after 15 years of offering bed-and-breakfast, has a coterie of regular guests. We can understand why they return to this large brick house, built in about 1870 in a 'Victorian-imitating-Georgian' style. Inside, every room is different, but all feel light and bright, thanks to large windows. Antiques, paintings and high-quality fabrics abound, while vases of flowers, skilfully arranged by Mrs Duke add an extra touch of elegance. Those who worry about the smells and sounds of farm animals need not be put off by the nearby barns, since the hub of the working farm is now one mile away.

Nearby Duxford Aircraft Museum, Audley End, golf.

Directions 2 miles W of Saffron Walden. Between villages of Littlebury and Elmdon. Get detailed directions.

Littlebury Green, Nr Saffron Walden, Essex CB11 4XB
Tel and Fax (01763) 838237
Location in huge country estate; ample car parking
Evening meal by request
Prices £££
Rooms 3 double; 1 single; all have TV, hairdrier, tea/coffee kit
Facilities sitting-room, dining-room; garden
Smoking permitted

Credit cards DC, MC, V
Children not suitable
Disabled not suitable
Pets no
Closed Christmas
Languages English only
Proprietor Mrs Diana Duke

East Anglia and The East Midlands

Saxlingham Thorpe, S of Norwich

The Lodge at Saxlingham

Some would describe this 18th-century house as being 'in the middle of nowhere', but that is the appeal for many guests. Some regulars stay for a week or more in summer. With Norwich only minutes away along the A140, however, owner Sally Dixon, like so many top-class bed-and-breakfast hosts, is welcoming more and more business people. Women in particular appreciate the advantages of staying in a real home, rather than a faceless hotel. Since she is also a Cordon Bleu cook, guests do not have to leave her elegant home in the evening. Imaginative dinners, based on local produce and her own herbs, are a candlelit affair.

Sally, who is self-assured, with a genuine welcome, has collected a variety of awards since she opened the Lodge to visitors. There is much to praise, particularly the three acres of splendid gardens, with the croquet lawn and neat flower beds. Inside, antiques fill the handsome Regency rooms, including the guests' own sitting-room. The bedrooms justify the tag of 'luxurious'. All in all, guests are happy to pay high prices to enjoy such comforts and to have such an aimiable family as hosts.

Nearby Norfolk Broads, the coast.
Directions 6 miles S of Norwich. Get final directions.

Cargate Lane, Saxlingham Thorpe, Norwich NR15 1TU
Tel (01508) 471422
Fax (01508) 471682
Location on edge of village; ample car parking
Evening meal by request
Prices £££-££££
Rooms 2 double; 1 single; all have radio, hairdrier, tea/coffee kit
Facilities sitting-room, dining-room; garden
Smoking outdoors only

Credit cards no
Children not suitable
Disabled not suitable
Pets no
Closed Christmas, New Year
Languages English only
Proprietors Sally and Roger Dixon

East Anglia and The East Midlands

Southwold

Acton Lodge

Southwold is 'prim perfection, a fine example of a genteel seaside town,' according to our inspector, who rates it one of the prettiest anywhere. Pastel blue and pink houses line the streets, while the beach huts must be the best-kept in the country. Overlooking South Green and the sea, among fishermen's cottages and Georgian mansions, stands Acton Lodge, an extravagant Victorian house topped with a square turret. Here, 'lovingly restored' hardly credits the hours Brenda Smith spent uncovering the original fruit and leaf plaster mouldings. She emphasized the Victorian ambience with heavy dark gold curtains and a huge yucca plant in the dining-room. In the sitting-room, the upright piano is well used by the actors who book in during Southwold's summer theatre season.

Don't expect the same decoration in the bedrooms, which are simpler, though comfortable enough. The most fun is the Turret Room, reached through a trapdoor in the ceiling which affords total privacy when closed. From here, views across town to the lighthouse and straight out to sea are magical.

Nearby Dunwich, Aldburgh; bird reserves; Norfolk Broads.
Directions on South Green near seafront.

18 South Green, Southwold, Suffolk IP18 6HB
Tel (01502) 723217
Location in heart of town; public (free) car parking
Evening meal no
Prices ££
Rooms 3 double; 1 single; all have TV, radio, hairdrier, tea/coffee kit
Facilities sitting-room, dining-room, library
Smoking outdoors only
Credit cards no

Children over 6
Disabled not suitable
Pets no
Closed never
Languages Polish
Proprietor Brenda Smith

East Anglia and The East Midlands

Thompson, NE of Thetford

College Farm

Stay here and, along with bed-and-breakfast, you get 650 years of history. We found this house fascinating. Dating back to 1349, it was built as a college, whose master and five priests served in a nearby chapel. The clerics would still recognize the great oak beams and church-style windows, but the panelling in the dining-room would be unfamiliar. That's because it was added 300 years later, in the 17thC. Around that time, the Garniers arrived from France, part of the tide of Huguenots who left when the Protestant religion was outlawed. The stories of the Garniers and College Farm merged in 1975 when the family bought what was a ruin and began renovations. Now, it is furnished with heavy oak furniture and hung with paintings. Although prices here are attractive, College Farm would not suit everyone. It has no sitting-room for guests, bathrooms are squeezed into quirky spaces, and the kitchen is a chaotic tumble of paperwork. However, we enjoyed the history, the village of Thetford, and meeting Lavender Garnier.

Nearby Norfolk Rural Life Museum, Lynford Arboretum.
Directions 12 miles NE of Thetford. Take A1075 for East Dereham. Turn off for Thompson. Get final directions.

Thompson, Thetford, Norfolk IP24 1QG **Tel** (01953) 483318 **Location** on edge of hamlet in own grounds; ample car parking **Evening meal** no **Prices** £ **Rooms** 3 double; all have TV, radio **Facilities** dining-room; garden **Smoking** permitted **Credit cards** no	**Children** over 7 **Disabled** not suitable **Pets** no **Closed** never **Languages** some French **Proprietor** Lavender Garnier

East Anglia and The East Midlands

Uggeshall, NW of Southwold

Uggeshall Manor Farm

Offering the best of both worlds, Uggeshall Manor Farm is surrounded by seemingly endless meadows, yet is only five minutes' drive from Southwold, one of England's prettiest seaside towns. From the 17thC pink brick farmhouse, which stands on a large pond, there are numerous fine walks. "Guests with dogs love to explore the six miles of conservation paths on the estate," according to Annie Davies. Her family breeds and shows horses, though visitors are equally intrigued by the classic cars which are her husband's hobby. Open only since 1998, the house has three guest-rooms that are fresh and bright, furnished with brass beds and attractive old, rather than heirloom, furniture. One has Victorian mahogany, another pine. The third, a twin-bedded room, has the advantage of its own small sitting-room, and down a few steps, a bathroom dominated by a Victorian roll-top tub.

Mrs Davies is particular about her breakfasts, including free-range eggs and "properly-cured local bacon". Although she does not offer an evening meal, she is happy to recommend three good pubs, all within a five minute drive.

Nearby Southwold, the sea.
Directions off A12, near Wangford. Get final directions.

Uggeshall, Near Wangford, Suffolk NR34 8BD	**Credit cards** no
Tel (01502) 578546	**Children** over 10
Fax (01502) 578560	**Disabled** not suitable
Location on large farm; ample car parking	**Pets** yes
Evening meal no	**Closed** Christmas
Prices £££	**Languages** English only
Rooms 3 double; all have TV, radio, hairdrier, tea/coffee kit	**Proprietor** Annie Davies
Facilities sitting-room, dining-room; garden	
Smoking outdoors only	

East Anglia and The East Midlands

Waterbeach, N of Cambridge

Berry House

Most guests stay in this 200-year-old house because it stands in a quiet village close to Cambridge and Ely. We would stay here for the food and touches of luxury. Sally Myburgh, a professional caterer, makes the evening meal 'something of an occasion'. She cures her own gravadlax and is keen on using local game, such as pheasant and quail. The well-priced four-course dinner is only available for two or more guests; otherwise, a simpler supper is served, or there are nearby restaurants. Sally takes just as much trouble over breakfast: choose between traditional English or a South-African-style start to the day, with exotic fruits.

The bonus of Berry House is its privacy. The original coach house is now the guest wing, where bedrooms in the former hayloft reflect Sally's exacting standards. The African Room, for example, has precisely matched colours and a bathroom with a 5-inch shower head and heavy brass fittings. Downstairs, guests have use of a sitting-room and kitchen which opens into the garden where golf enthusiast Phil Myburgh has recently installed a tiny putting course.

Nearby Cambridge, Ely, Newmarket, Anglesey Abbey.
Directions 3 miles N of Cambridge. Take A10 for Ely.

High Street, Waterbeach, Cambridge CB5 9JU	**Smoking** permitted
Tel (01223) 860702	**Credit cards** no
Fax (01223) 570588	**Children** welcome
Location in quiet village; ample car parking	**Disabled** not suitable
Evening meal by request	**Pets** yes
Prices ££–£££	**Closed** never
Rooms 2 double; all have radio, hairdrier, tea/coffee kit	**Languages** French, Spanish, Afrikaans
Facilities sitting/dining-room; garden, golf putting green, croquet	**Proprietors** Phil and Sally Myburgh

➡ *More on page 158*

The Cotswolds and The Midlands

Broadway

Barn House

'I did not expect to find a bed-and-breakfast like this, right in the heart of Broadway,' was the honest admission of our inspector.

Although Barn House faces the main street of this well-known Cotswold village, behind it stretch 16 acres of gardens and paddocks. The manicured lawns, with flowering shrubs and borders, are an attraction in their own right, open to the public through the National Gardens Scheme. The large house was renovated in 1703 but is much older, 'though we don't have the full history,' Jane Ricketts admits. With classic English under-statement, she calls the main bedroom the 'big double'. Spacious enough to swallow up the king-size bed, it also has its own dressing-room and large bathroom. The two other rooms are smaller but equally comfortable.

Downstairs, the original barn is a dramatic two-storey sitting-room, with a grand piano that guests are invited to play. Add in the 42-foot indoor swimming-pool and you have a gem. Although afternoon teas are served to the public in the garden in the summer, this does not spoil the ambience.

Nearby Cotswold villages, Cotswold Way trail.
Directions on main street of village.

---

152 High Street, Broadway, Worcestershire WR12 7AJ
Tel and Fax (01386) 858633
Location in heart of village; own car parking
Evening meal no
Prices ££–££££
Rooms 4 double; all have TV, radio, hairdrier, tea/coffee kit
Facilities 2 sitting-rooms, dining-room; garden, indoor heated swimming-pool
Smoking restricted

Credit cards no
Children welcome
Disabled not suitable
Pets kennels, stables, paddocks by arrangement
Closed never
Languages English only
Proprietor Jane Ricketts

The Cotswolds and The Midlands

Clun, W of Craven Arms

Cockford Hall

Roger Wren is a restaurateur, who made his name with Walton's, the English House, the English Garden and the Lindsay House, all in London. This venture, however, is deep in the idyllic Shropshire countryside. Cockford Hall sounds like a grand mansion; in fact, it is a rather plain-looking Georgian farmhouse, now transformed into a luxury retreat.

As in the best hotels, the light-switch is right by the bed, while bathrooms have large baths as well as separate, roomy showers. There are only two bedrooms in the house; each has antiques plus a state-of-the-art, individual sound system for listening to everything from CDs to BBC Radio 4. Yet the style remains personal rather than formal, with amusing touches of whimsy, such as a hand-sewn Egyptian rug with colourful birds.

In a separate building, the Dick Turpin cottage, new in 1997, allows total privacy. On the hillside behind, 4,000 trees plus wildflowers have been planted, to create a garden that is 'anything but suburban'. Expect fine food, total quiet and prices that are surprisingly reasonable for this type of quality.

Nearby Clun, Stokesay Castle, Ludlow; walking, riding.

Directions 8 miles W of Craven Arms. Get final directions.

Clun, Shropshire SY7 8LR	**Children** not suitable
Tel (01588) 640327	**Disabled** not suitable
Fax (01588) 640881	**Pets** no
Location in hillside meadows; ample car parking	**Closed** never
Evening meal by request	**Languages** German
Prices ££–££££	**Proprietor** Roger Wren
Rooms 2 double; 1 suite; all have telephone, TV, radio, hairdrier, tea/coffee kit	
Facilities sitting-room, dining-room; garden	
Smoking restricted	
Credit cards no	

The Cotswolds and The Midlands

Diddlebury, E of Craven Arms

Delbury Hall

'Stately', 'grand' and 'imposing' are the adjectives that come to mind when describing Delbury Hall. Swans glide serenely across the ornamental lake, roses and honeysuckle climb over an arbour by the tennis court and even the stables and carriage house look impressive. Not far from the house is a fishery, stocked with rainbow and brown trout. Built in 1753, the Hall has been in the Wrigley family for 80 years. Despite the antiques and portraits, the ambience is not formal. "Far from it. After all, we have two small children," is Patrick Wrigley's explanation. An ex-army-officer and amateur jockey, he is also an inventive cook, whose menus may include seafood soup or *gravadlax* with *blinis*, local lamb or game in season.

Although children are welcome to stay, they are given an early supper; the silver and crystal in the dining-room are reserved for adults. This is not for anyone on a budget. Prices are right at the top of the range, but then this is a special experience. Where else can you wake up in a private mansion, gaze out over the Shropshire Hills and pretend that it is all yours?

Nearby Stokesay Castle, Ludlow, Much Wenlock; walking.
Directions 6 miles E of Craven Arms. Get final directions.

Diddlebury, Craven Arms, Shropshire SY7 9DH
Tel (01584) 841267
Fax (01584) 841441
E-mail wrigley@delbury.demon.co.uk
Location outside village, in own grounds; ample car parking
Evening meal by request
Prices ££££
Rooms 3 double; all have telephone, TV, radio, tea/coffee kit
Facilities 2 sitting-rooms, dining-room; garden, tennis court, fishery
Smoking restricted
Credit cards MC, V
Children welcome
Disabled not suitable
Pets no
Closed Christmas
Languages some French
Proprietors Lucinda and Patrick Wrigley

The Cotswolds and The Midlands

Laverton Meadows, SW of Broadway

Leasow House

Gordon and Barbara Meekings have been welcoming guests into their home since 1985, far longer than most hosts in this book. Behind their 16thC Cotswold stone farmhouse are stables and barns, which have been sympathetically and stylishly converted for guests. We were pleased to see that The Bull Pen, decorated in a cheerful red and white theme, has been partially adapted for wheelchair-users. Up above is the Hayloft. With its exposed stone walls, steeply pitched roof and little balcony, this is a favourite for a romantic occasion.

There are five more rooms in the main house. These vary in style and size but do not have the priceless antiques and expensive furnishings of some houses. All, however, are comfortable, with views over quiet surrounding farmland.

Leasow House is a practical and popular base for touring. Although it could feel busy when full, breakfast is served at separate tables, so guests don't have to be sociable first thing in the morning. Barbara Meekings is an experienced hostess, who succeeds in creating an informal, relaxing atmosphere.

Nearby Cotswold Hills, Cheltenham, gardens; walking, cycling.
Directions 2 miles SW of Broadway. Get final directions.

Laverton Meadows,
Broadway, Worcestershire
WR12 7NA
Tel (01386) 584526
Fax (01386) 584596
E-mail leasow@clara.net
Location in open countryside;
ample car parking
Evening meal no
Prices £££
Rooms 7 double; all have TV,
hairdrier, tea/coffee kit
Facilities sitting-room, dining-
room; garden

Smoking outdoors only
Credit cards AE, MC, V
Children welcome
Disabled access to 1 room
Pets by arrangement
Closed never
Languages English only
Proprietors Barbara and
Gordon Meekings

The Cotswolds and The Midlands

Cardynham House

With its handsome 15thC church and gabled cottages, the mellow stone town of Painswick is much more than a base for exploring the Cotswolds. Thanks to a natural talent for design and colour, Carol Keyes' five-hundred-year old home is one of the most striking in this entire book. In less than a decade, this lively painter and sculptor has transformed a derelict house into a home that is featured in glossy interior design magazines.

The names of the bedrooms give a clue: Arabian Nights, New England and The Highlands. We like the medieval charm of Old Tuscany, enhanced by thick fabrics; English Garden is filled with floral prints; while The Dovecot is a magical combination of dark beams and pure white drapes on the four-poster. At the same time, Carol's American roots ensure every contemporary convenience, from television to central heating. Breakfasts, too, might include transatlantic pancakes or waffles. Carol allows a Thai restaurant to operate in the March Hare room on the ground floor from Wednesday to Saturday (evenings): a unique contribution to this book.

Nearby the Cotswold hills and villages.

Directions 3 miles N of Stroud, in middle of town.

The Cross, Painswick, Stroud GL6 6XX	**Credit cards** no
Tel (01452) 814006	**Children** welcome
Fax (01452) 812321	**Disabled** not suitable
Location in middle of town; car parking on street	**Pets** no
Evening meal no	**Closed** Christmas
Prices ££££	**Languages** some French
Rooms 9 double; all have telephone, TV, radio, hairdrier, tea/coffee kit	**Proprietor** Carol Keyes
Facilities sitting-room, dining-room; garden	
Smoking outdoors only	

The Cotswolds and The Midlands

St Briavels, N of Chepstow

Cinderhill House

When the English live abroad, this is the sort of cottage they dream of, complete with an inglenook fireplace, beams to bump your head on and a history of nearly 700 years. There are even roses climbing above the doorway. Since our first visit in 1987, this has been a favourite hideaway, as much for the prettily decorated rooms as for Gillie Peacock's meals. She is a professional cook, whose dinners outshine the 'dinner-party' fare served in most upmarket bed-and-breakfasts. As well as the 'traditional English' breakfast, she offers a herb omelette or, perhaps, fresh salmon fish cakes. We stay in the main house for the full atmosphere, despite small bathrooms tucked into odd spaces. Those preferring more privacy can book into one of the cottages in the large garden.

The village of St Briavels (rhymes with 'revels') boasts a small castle, built long ago to keep out the Welsh. Today, the view across the Wye valley to Wales is totally peaceful, the stillness broken only by birdsong.

Nearby Tintern Abbey, Offa's Dyke Path, Forest of Dean.
Directions 6 miles N of Chepstow. Take B4228 to St Briavels. Get final directions.

St Briavels, Gloucestershire
GL15 6RH
Tel (01594) 530393
Fax (01594) 530098
Location on hillside
overlooking Wye Valley; own
car parking
Evening meal by request
Prices £££
Rooms 5 double; all have
tea/coffee kit
Facilities sitting-room, dining-room; garden, terrace
Smoking outdoors only

Credit cards no
Children welcome
Disabled not suitable
Pets no
Closed Jan
Languages English only
Proprietor Gillie Peacock

The Cotswolds and The Midlands

Whitchurch

Dearnford Hall

We have inspected farmhouses all over the UK, from the small and cosy to the grand and imposing. Dearnford Hall strikes a happy medium. Although the late-17thC house is large, with high ceilings, spacious rooms and antiques, there is nothing formal about the atmosphere.

This has been the Bebbington home for over 30 years, 'though my uncle lived here before your family bought it,' Jane Bebbington reminds her husband, Charles, with her ready smile. She is the sort of cheerful hostess who makes guests feel at ease immediately. In the morning, she puts coffee in the dining-room before breakfast, 'because the smell is so inviting' and chooses background music, perhaps Vivaldi or English folk songs. The two bedrooms are spacious and well furnished; bathrooms are modern.

The house stands in a working farm of 300 acres, which includes a fishery. This spring-fed lake is stocked with rainbow, brown and even brook trout, to challenge the fly-fisherman. There is also salmon fishing nearby on the River Dee.

Nearby Welsh hills, Chester, Erddig, The Potteries.
Directions 2 miles SW of Whitchurch. Get final directions.

Whitchurch, Shropshire
SY13 3JJ
Tel (01948) 662319
Fax (01948) 666670
Location in open farmland, not far from A41; ample car parking
Evening meal no
Prices ££££
Rooms 2 double; all have TV, radio, hairdrier, tea/coffee kit
Facilities sitting-room, dining-room; garden, trout fishing

Smoking outdoors only
Credit cards no
Children not suitable
Disabled not suitable
Pets no
Closed Christmas
Languages English only
Proprietors Charles and Jane Bebbington

The Cotswolds and The Midlands

Willersey, N of Broadway

The Old Rectory

The Cotswold Hills are dotted with villages that truly deserve the description 'picturesque'. Many visitors stop only in well-known places such as Broadway, Chipping Campden, Stow-on-the-Wold and The Slaughters. There are, however, plenty of hamlets that remain undisturbed by coaches and tourist traffic.

Willersey is one of these. With a green, a pub and a Norman church, it has all the prerequisites of a classic English country village. In 1994, the Beauvoisins took over what was already a popular bed-and-breakfast and have upgraded furnishings and bathrooms. Don't expect an away-from-it-all atmosphere: with eight bedrooms, this is larger than most establishments in this book. It is useful, however, for those who find stairs a problem, since two of the bedrooms are on the ground floor of the converted coach house.

The garden is delightful and Liz makes breakfast an occasion. Some may be put off by the guidelines on when to arrive, the extra charge for high season and the Crabtree and Evelyn toiletries that are for sale. Let us know what you think.

Nearby Cotswold villages, Cotswold Way trail, Cheltenham.
Directions 1.5 miles N of Broadway. Get final directions.

Church Street, Willersey, Nr Broadway, Worcestershire WR12 7PN
Tel (01386) 853729
Fax (01386) 858061
E-mail beauvoisin@btinternet.com
Location by church in quiet village; own car parking
Evening meal no
Prices £££–££££
Rooms 8 double; all have telephone, TV, radio, hairdrier, tea/coffee kit
Facilities dining-room; terrace, garden
Smoking outdoors only
Credit cards MC, V
Children over 8
Disabled not suitable
Pets no
Closed Christmas
Languages French, German
Proprietor Liz Beauvoisin

➡ *More on page 162*

North Wales

Bala

Fron Feuno Hall

After a more than a decade of welcoming guests, running a bed and breakfast can become just another business. Not for Mair Reeves, an outgoing hostess who has never lost her enthusiasm and sense of fun. Regulars return year after year to the spacious family home standing high on a hill above Lake Bala. In spring, the garden blooms with daffodils, tulips and rhododendron; summer brings the scent of roses and wisteria, which climb along the front of the house. In fine weather, guests can breakfast on the terrace, eating eggs from the Reeves' own chickens and guinea fowl. Dinner could be a light supper or a three-course meal. "I'm a straightforward country cook," Mair explains; but, as well as roast pork and beef, she enjoys preparing spicy dishes that recall the years she and her husband, Jack, spent living in the Far East. Bedrooms vary from the smallest, which has a cottagey-feel, to the large Blue Room, with a four-poster bed and yards of white lace. All, however, face the lake. There is croquet on the lawn and also a tennis court, with rackets for guests to borrow.

Nearby Bodnant Gardens, castles, walking, sailing, golf.
Directions 2 miles SW of Bala on north shore of the lake.

Bala, Gwynedd LL23 7YF
Tel (01678) 521115
Fax (01678) 521151
Location in gardens above lake; ample car parking
Evening meal by request
Prices ££££
Rooms 3 double; all have radio, hairdrier, tea/coffee kit
Facilities sitting-room, dining-room; garden, tennis court, croquet
Smoking restricted

Credit cards no
Children not suitable
Disabled not suitable
Pets yes
Closed Nov to March
Languages Welsh
Proprietors Mair and Jack Reeves

South Wales

Brecon

Cantre Selyf

As the main gateway to the Brecon Beacon National Park, Brecon has long been a popular base for outdoors-lovers. Now, the old market town is getting a new lease of life. Georgian and Victorian buildings are being repainted, the jazz festival is an international affair and a brand new theatre opened in 1997.

Cantre Selyf is top of our list of places to stay in Brecon. Located right in the heart of town, it is handy for the cathedral and museums. Although the front door faces the street, the three bedrooms are at the back, ensuring a quiet night's sleep. Unlike some hosts, who err on the side of over-decoration, Helen Roberts keeps it simple, putting white duvets on iron bedsteads and choosing easy-on-the-eye wallpaper. Downstairs, a bold red carpet accentuates the dramatic black and white Jacobean entrance hall, with its 300-year-old carved staircase. Behind the house, the surprisingly large garden makes a peaceful spot for unwinding at the end of the day. Well-priced evening meals feature local produce such as wild salmon from the nearby River Usk or Welsh lamb with an elderberry and port sauce.

Nearby museums; Brecon Beacons; fishing, golf.
Directions Lion Street is between the High Street and the TIC.

---

5 Lion Street, Brecon, Powys LD3 7AU
Tel (01874) 622904
Fax (01874) 622315
E-mail cantreselyf@imaginet.co.uk
Location in heart of old town; own car parking
Evening meal by request
Prices ££
Rooms 3 double; all have radio, hairdrier, tea/coffee kit
Facilities sitting-room, dining-room; garden

Smoking outdoors only
Credit cards no
Children welcome
Disabled not suitable
Pets no
Closed Christmas
Languages French
Proprietors Helen and Nigel Roberts

South Wales

Spring Farm

One of William Wordsworth's best-loved poems is 'Lines composed a few miles above Tintern Abbey'. Two hundred years later, the lofty views from Spring Farm are still as inspirational. The ruins of Tintern stand in the valley below, just out of sight around a curve in the River Wye. Beyond glints the River Severn and in the distance rise the Mendip Hills. Sheep grazing in the meadows complete the idyllic scene.

This is no workaday farm. Well-tended gardens and lawns surround the 300-year-old house, which Logan and Julia Hunter have spent the last 20 years renovating. They added the conservatory, growing winter jasmine for fragrance and bougainvillea for colour. Candlelit in the evening, guests can relax here or, in fine weather, on the terrace outside.

The Logans have offered hospitality for two decades, but this is still very much the family home. Regulars return to explore the ten nearby castles and to walk the Offa's Dyke Path, which passes right by the farm.

Nearby Tintern Abbey, Forest of Dean, Brecon Beacons.
Directions 6 miles N of Chepstow. Take A466 to Monmouth. After Tintern, turn right to Brockweir. Get final directions.

Brockweir, Chepstow, Gwent NP6 7NU
Tel and Fax (01291) 689439
Location on hillside above Wye Valley; ample car parking
Evening meal by request
Prices £££
Rooms 2 double; all have radio, tea/coffee kit
Facilities sitting-room, dining-room; garden
Smoking outdoors only
Credit cards no

Children over 10
Disabled not suitable
Pets no
Closed Nov to Easter
Languages English only
Proprietors Julia and Logan Hunter

South Wales

Erwood, SE of Builth Wells

Pwll-Y-Faedda

Standing on the banks of the River Wye, this gracious house was built in 1922 as a fishing lodge for an aristocrat. The difficult-to-pronounce name, shortened to 'Poolly' by locals, refers to the main pool on this stretch of water. Jeremy Jaquet is a fly-fisherman, and guests who share his enthusiasm can cast for salmon and trout on his mile-long beat. Arrangements can be made for a gillie or tuition. He and his American wife, Yolande, spent many years in the Middle and Far East; having decided to offer bed-and-breakfast, they told their friends in far-flung places. That was in 1997; since then, visitors from the United States, Australia and New Zealand, as well as China, India, Japan and South America have found their way to this luxurious home, furnished with family photographs and mementoes of their travels. Yolande is a keen cook, always trying new recipes from her library of over one hundred books. Her four-course meals end with coffee and chocolates in the spacious sitting-room. Upstairs, the three bedrooms are prettily-decorated, but there is also a conservatory and pool room.

Nearby walking, Hay-on-Wye.

Directions 7 miles SE of Builth Wells. Get final decorations.

Erwood, Builth Wells, Powys LD2 3YS
Tel (01982) 560202
Fax (01982) 560732
E-mail yolande@btinternet.com.uk
Location on River Wye; ample car parking
Evening meal by request
Prices £££
Rooms 3 double; all have radio, hairdrier, tea/coffee kit
Facilities sitting-room, dining-room, conservatory, pool room; garden, fishing
Smoking restricted
Credit cards MC, V
Children over 12
Disabled not suitable
Pets by arrangement
Closed Nov to end-Feb
Languages some French, German
Proprietors Yolande and Jeremy Jaquet

Mid-Wales

Garthmyl Hall

We admire the enthusiasm of Tim and Nancy Morrow. We also applaud their design skills. In 1995, this young couple bought a ruin and transformed it into a mansion fit for a glossy-magazine feature. Everything here is on a grand scale, from the hand-painted coffered ceilings to enormous gilt mirrors and deep purple velvet curtains. Each bedroom follows a different theme. In the Egyptian Room, for example, sphinx carvings decorate the high-standing French Empire bed, with steps ready for climbing up at night. Bathrooms are luxurious, especially the towels. Even the garden is impressive.

Some might argue that, with nine bedrooms, this a small hotel. Tim Morrow disagrees. "After all, we are the hosts, we do the cooking and this is our home." Their down-to-earth attitude offsets the inherent formality of this house. Prices vary according to the size of the room. Some are high, though we think they are justified; the lower rates are notable value. There is a road in front, but it does not spoil views across the valley.

Nearby Montgomery, Powis Castle, Offa's Dyke, River Severn.
Directions 4 miles NW of Montgomery. Take B4385. Turn left on A483. House is on the right.

Garthmyl, nr Montgomery
SY15 6RS
Tel (01686) 640550
Fax (01686) 640609
Location in extensive grounds with formal gardens; ample car parking
Evening meal by request
Prices £££–££££
Rooms 9 double; all have tea/coffee kit; TV by request
Facilities sitting-room, dining-room; garden
Smoking restricted

Credit cards MC, V
Children very welcome
Disabled not suitable
Pets no
Closed never
Languages some French
Proprietors Nancy and Tim Morrow

North Wales

Llandudno

The Lighthouse

'The most dramatic setting for any bed-and-breakfast I've ever seen' read the report on The Lighthouse, at the far end of the Great Orme's Head promontory. A sheer cliff drops 360 feet down to the rocks; due north across the Irish Sea is the Isle of Man. Most lighthouses are utilitarian structures; this is a flight of Victorian fantasy. The outside looks like a castle; the interior resembles an ocean liner, with panels of polished wood.

From 1862 to 1985, the light flashed from the panoramic windows of what is now the Lamp Room Suite. Today, guests sit back and watch ships sailing to and from Liverpool, and spot razorbills, kittiwakes and guillemots. Above, the Telegraph Room feels like a captain's cabin: sit in bed and you have a stunning view out of each of the six windows. The outlook from the Principal Keeper's Suite is less impressive, but its two bedrooms make it useful for families. The only drawback is that host John Callin does not offer dinner. Llandudno is only a short drive away, but care is needed for the return journey at night along the narrow cliff road.

Nearby Conwy, Snowdonia National Park.
Directions 2 miles NW of Llandudno. Get directions.

Marine Drive, Great Orme's Head, Llandudno, Conwy LL30 2XD
Tel and Fax (01492) 876819
E-mail lighthouse.gb@dial.pipex.com
Location on headland, overlooking sea; ample car parking
Evening meal no
Prices ££££
Rooms 3 suites; all have TV, binoculars
Facilities dining-room; garden

Smoking outdoors only
Credit cards no
Children very welcome
Disabled not suitable
Pets no
Closed never
Languages some French
Proprietor John Callin

Mid-Wales

Llanegryn, NE of Tywyn

Peniarth Uchaf

Wales is full of secret valleys accessible only by narrow back roads. The Dysynni Valley is one of the prettiest, only 5 miles inland from Cardigan Bay and right in Snowdonia National Park. Once past the uninspiring village of Llanegryn, the lane winds through verdant meadows that contrast with the rocky hills. Beneath one craggy escarpment stands this spacious house, that has been in the Corbett family since it was built in 1818.

After an army career that included postings to Singapore, Hong Kong and Borneo, Norman and Alison Corbett returned to this quiet clearing in the woods. There is no military stiffness about them, however, and Alison has a quick, jolly laugh that puts guests at ease right away. She sends birdwatchers off to spot red kites, walkers to a nearby ruined castle, and hikers to climb up Cader Idris, nearly 3,000 feet high. Those with energy left can play tennis, while others relax on the terrace or in the drawing-room, with its old family portraits and photographs. Expect homey comforts, 'dinner-party' food and a sound sleep.

Nearby Centre for Alternative Technology, Talyllyn Railway.
Directions 7 miles from Tywyn. Take A493 through Bryncrug to Llanegryn. Get final directions.

Llanegryn, Tywyn, Gwynedd LL36 9UG
Tel (01654) 710804
Fax (01654) 712044
Location in secluded woodland clearing; ample car parking
Evening meal by request
Prices £££
Rooms 3 double; all have radio, hairdrier, tea/coffee kit
Facilities sitting-room, dining-room; garden, tennis court

Smoking outdoors only
Credit cards no
Children over 12
Disabled not suitable
Pets no
Closed Christmas, New Year, Easter
Languages Swahili, Gurkhali
Proprietors Norman and Alison Corbett

North Wales

Llanerchymedd, Isle of Anglesey

Llwydiarth Fawr

The longest place-name in the world is the Welsh town of Llanfairpwllgwyngyllgogerychwyrndrobwllllantysiliogogogoch. Some holidaymakers drive across the Menai Bridge to the island of Anglesey just to photograph the sign at the railway station. Others carry straight on for Holyhead, to catch the ferry to Ireland. They miss out on a castle, a stately home, bird reserves and empty lanes for cycling.

For those who stay, Llwydiarth Fawr makes a fine base. The spacious early-19thC house was originally the home of an affluent shipbuilder. Surrounded by 850 acres, this is a place for those who want a 'get away from it all' break. Rooms downstairs combine antiques and family collectibles; the comfortable bedrooms are in cheerful colours. The Hughes have handed over the running of the farm to their sons, so Margaret can concentrate on her guests. Her evening meals often feature highly acclaimed Anglesey lamb. Since the farm animals are well away from the house, sensitive city-folk are not offended by their sounds and smells.

Nearby Beaumaris castle; sea, water sports.
Directions 14 miles from Menai Bridge. Get final directions.

Llanerchymedd, Isle of Anglesey, Gwynedd LL71 8DF
Tel (01248) 470321
Location in rural heart of the island; ample car parking
Evening meal by request
Prices ££
Rooms 3 double; all have TV, radio, hairdrier, tea/coffee kit
Facilities sitting-room, dining-room; garden, terrace, lake for private fishing
Smoking outdoors only

Credit cards MC, V
Children very welcome
Disabled not suitable
Pets no
Closed Christmas
Languages Welsh
Proprietors Margaret and Richard Hughes

North Wales

Cyfie Farm

It is worth the effort to find this farm, deep in the middle of nowhere. The peak of Cadair Berwyn rises to the north, with Cader Idris to the west, while smaller ridges and valleys rollercoaster away to the south. Roads, railways and pylons have been banished from the landscape.

After welcoming guests for 20 years, some hosts become jaded. Not Lynn and George Jenkins, who have kept up their enthusiasm as well as their standards. Their 17thC Welsh longhouse is just that, long and thin, with small rooms and a truly cosy atmosphere. We were impressed by the suites in the recently converted stable block, with their distinctive colours and patterns. Dinners, too, are something special, with dishes such as fresh asparagus soufflé and wild blackberry brûlée. Regulars book in for a week, going off for the day to Lake Vyrnwy and Snowdonia. Bracken, the Welsh border collie, likes taking guests for a walk but we would be content to sit in the garden, gaze at the view and do nothing at all.

Nearby Lake Vyrnwy, Welsh uplands.
Directions 13 miles NW of Welshpool. Take A490 to Llanfyllin. Difficult to find. Get directions.

Llanfihangel, Llanfyllin,
Powys SY22 5JE
Tel and Fax (01691) 648451
Location on remote hilltop;
ample car parking
Evening meal by request
Prices ££
Rooms 1 double; 3 suites; all
have TV, radio, hairdrier,
tea/coffee kit, refrigerator
Facilities sitting-room, dining-room; garden
Smoking outdoors only
Credit cards no

Children very welcome
Disabled not suitable
Pets no
Closed never
Languages English only
Proprietors George and Lynn
Jenkins

South Wales

Llanfihangel Cruc., N of Abergavenny

Penyclawdd Court

There are numerous medieval buildings in Britain. Some have been converted to hotels, others offer 'Tudor banquets'. Penyclawdd Court is different. Never have we seen a 'time machine' as genuine as this. The interior is surprisingly sombre, thanks to small windows, low ceilings and dark wood beams. All year long, logs burn in the enormous fireplace. This is the 'modern wing', added in 1625; the dining-room was built around 1480. Here, Julia Evans and Ken Peacock serve candlelit dinners recreating Tudor recipes such as hare in ale with saffron. Of the four bedrooms, our favourite is the Oak Room. This overlooks the garden, with its roses, honeysuckle and the earthworks of a Norman fortress at the far end.

This is an experience unlike any other. Although modern comforts such as electricity, under-floor heating and bathrooms have been installed, these seem almost like intrusions from the 20thC. We found it all fascinating but cannot recommend it for everyone. For some, the step back in time may be too dramatic.

Nearby Brecon Beacons, Offa's Dyke Path, Big Pit Mine.
Directions 5 miles N of Abergavenny. Take A465 N to Llanfihangel Crucorney. Get final directions.

Llanfihangel Crucorney, Nr Abergavenny, Monmouthshire NP7 7LB
Tel (01873) 890719
Fax (01873) 890848
Location in extensive grounds at end of badly rutted drive; ample car parking
Evening meal by request
Prices ££££
Rooms 4 double; all have TV, tea/coffee kit
Facilities sitting-room, dining-room; garden

Smoking restricted
Credit cards MC, V
Children over 12
Disabled not suitable
Pets no
Closed never
Languages some French
Proprietors Julia Evans and Ken Peacock

North Wales

Llansilin, W of Oswestry

Glascoed Hall

A neatly clipped yew hedge 15 feet high and a manicured lawn signal that this Elizabethan manor is no ordinary 'working farm'. Tucked away in the formal gardens are a tennis court and a heated, outdoor swimming-pool. Even the tidy barns stand discreetly behind the house, facing away towards the valley, as if to shield guests from the animals.

Inside, rooms ooze with history. 'You feel like you've gone back 400 years,' according to one guest, 'particularly at night when firelight plays on the ancient carved oak beams and ornate staircase.' Comforts are pure 20thC, however, from secondary glazing to heated towel rails. Both bedrooms are well furnished: in one, plain white walls contrast with dark beams; the other is brightened by a cheery yellow-patterned bedcover.

Louise Howard-Baker is an ambitious cook and Ben's extensive wine list ranges from Australia to Burgundy and Bordeaux. By the end of the evening, 'you may feel as if you've drunk too much, but it's only the floors that slope with age.'

Nearby Llangollen; Offa's Dyke Path, Lake Vyrnwy; museums.
Directions 7 miles W of Oswestry. Take B4580 to Llansilin. Get final directions.

Llansilin, Nr Oswestry, Powys SY10 9BP
Tel (01691) 791334
Location deep in foothills of Welsh Borders; ample car parking
Evening meal by request
Prices £££
Rooms 2 double; all have radio, hairdrier, tea/coffee kit
Facilities 2 sitting-rooms, dining-room; garden, heated outdoor swimming-pool, tennis court
Smoking restricted
Credit cards MC, V
Children over 8
Disabled not suitable
Pets by arrangement
Closed Christmas, New Year
Languages French
Proprietors Ben and Louise Howard-Baker

North Wales

Pengwern Farm

Many of the hosts in this book decided to welcome guests once their children left home. Others fled the urban rat race, opting for the slower pace of country life. Jane and Gwyndaf Rowlands are different. Jane grew up on this extensive farm, now run by her brother. She and her husband, Gwyndaf, turned the family home into an award-winning bed-and-breakfast. We like this jolly team, who manage to look after their two boys as well as to cater for visitors. "He is the breakfast chef, I'm responsible for dinner," Jane explains with her infectious smile. Both are native Welsh-speakers who enjoy explaining the tongue-twisting language to foreigners.

They are not trying to compete with historic mansions full of priceless antiques. What they offer is a countryside setting handy for sightseeing and walking. Rooms are perfectly comfortable, not designer-decorated, but the modern bathrooms deserve commendation. Two are unusually spacious; the third has a Jacuzzi. A warning to late-rising city-folk: like all working farms, this has the early-morning sounds of tractors, sheep and cattle.

Nearby Caernarfon, Snowdonia National Park, beaches.
Directions 3 miles S of Caernarfon.

Saron, Llanwnda, Caernarfon, Gwynedd LL54 5UH	**Children** very welcome
	Disabled not suitable
	Pets no
Tel and Fax (01286) 831500	**Closed** Dec, Jan
Location in large farm near coast; ample car parking	**Languages** Welsh
	Proprietors Gwyndaf and Jane Rowlands
Evening meal by request	
Prices ££	
Rooms 3 double; all have TV, tea/coffee kit	
Facilities sitting-room, dining-room; garden	
Smoking outdoors only	
Credit cards no	

South Wales

Glasdir Bach

Landscape architect Wendy Beresford-Davies grew up nearby, moved away, but 'always wanted to come home'. We can see why; this hilltop deep in the Pembrokeshire National Park has wide-open views south to Carn Ingli, the mountain of the Angels. The sea is only two miles away. Along the coastal path are eagles and razorbills, as well as the breeding grounds for seals and puffins. In the hamlet of Nevern, down in the valley, a Celtic cross stands by the church, which dates back to the 6thC. Nearby, anglers cast for both salmon and trout in the river.

The first guests were welcomed to Glasdir Bach in 1997. They found a house that looks spacious but not grand, elegant but not formal. Don't expect the ambience of a bygone age: the building dates from 1810, but has been expanded over the years. On the ground floor, a sliding door leads to the honey-moon suite, with a large bathroom. One of the two bedrooms upstairs has views of the sea. Guests may use the all-weather tennis court.

Nearby Pembrokeshire Coastal Path; fishing, golf, water sports.
Directions 9 miles SW of Cardigan. Take A487 to Nevern. 1 mile from village. Get final directions.

Nevern, Nr Newport, Pembrokeshire SA42 0NO
Tel (01239) 820623
Location on a hilltop near the sea; ample car parking
Evening meal by arrangement
Prices ££
Rooms 3 double
Facilities sitting-room, dining-room; garden, terrace, tennis court
Smoking restricted
Credit cards MC, V
Children over 12

Disabled not suitable
Pets no
Closed Nov to Easter
Languages Norwegian
Proprietors Sydney and Wendy Beresford-Davies

North Wales

Penmachno, S of Betws-y-coed

Penmachno Hall

'If I have a night off with no guests, I invite the village in.'
Modwena Cutler has long been used to dispensing hospitality,
having run a pub and a restaurant in England before returning
to her Welsh roots in 1990. Some might call her theatrical with
her oversize glasses and funky earrings. Her husband, Ian, is tall
and more reserved, but has a laconic sense of humour. They
make delightful and thoughtful hosts, and know all the back
roads to hidden valleys and unspoiled, desolate hilltops.

Not for them the traditional look of so many upmarket bed-
and-breakfasts. Their Victorian rectory is hung with contemporary paintings and batiks from Modwena's years in the Far East.
They chose not to put televisions and telephones in the bedrooms, 'because that would spoil the atmosphere'. Regulars
enjoy the sociable atmosphere combined with the peaceful setting. Breakfast at 9 am is a communal affair, though anyone
needing a shot of caffeine earlier can have tea or coffee brought
to their room.

Nearby Snowdonia National Park, fishing, woollen mill.
Directions 5 miles S of Betws-y-coed. Take A5 south. Turn right
on to B4406 to Penmachno village. Get final directions.

Penmachno, Betws-y-coed,
North Wales LL24 OPU
Tel (01690) 760207
Location in large garden
outside tiny village; ample car
parking
Evening meal by request
Prices ££
Rooms 4 double
Facilities 3 sitting-rooms,
dining-room, conservatory;
garden
Smoking restricted
Credit cards MC, V

Children very welcome
Disabled not suitable
Pets no
Closed Christmas, New Year
Languages some French
Proprietors Modwena and
Ian Cutler

Mid-Wales

Rhydyfelin, SE of Aberystwyth

Nanteos Mansion

At the end of a long drive through extensive parkland, Nanteos Mansion stands on a hillside with wide-ranging views across fields of sheep. The foundation stone was laid in 1739 by Thomas Powell, whose descendants range from a Lord Lieutenant of Cardiganshire to ladies-in-waiting to Queen Victoria. There are romantic links with composer Richard Wagner, poet Lord Byron and even the Holy Grail. Rooms here are on a grand scale, from the enormous stone fireplace in the sitting-room to a carved staircase wide enough for old-fashioned crinoline skirts. Since 1997, a programme of much-needed refurbishment has transformed the house. Bedrooms that were plain and simple are now prettily-decorated in florals and chintz. The cheerful morning-room, at the front of the mansion, is a restaurant, open to non-residents as well as guests. Dinner here is a formal affair, but guests with children can request an early supper for youngsters under ten. With a long experience of running hotels and restaurants, the new hosts, Graham and Sue Hodgson-Jones, are helping Nanteos realize its full potential.

Nearby coast, walking, golf.
Directions 2 miles SE of Aberystwyth. Get final directions.

Rhydyfelin, Aberystwyth SY23 4LU	**Smoking** restricted
Tel (01970) 624363	**Credit cards** MC, V
Fax (01970) 626332	**Children** over 6
E-mail nanteos@btinternet.com	**Disabled** not suitable
Location in extensive parkland; ample car parking	**Pets** no
Evening meal yes	**Closed** Jan
Prices ££££	**Languages** some French
Rooms 6 double; all have TV, radio, hairdrier, tea/coffee kit	**Managers** Graham and Sue Hodgson-Jones
Facilities sitting-room, 2 dining-rooms, bar; garden	

Yorkshire

Askrigg, W of Leyburn

Helm

'You know Helm must be an away-from-it-all place when you turn on to a narrow lane marked 'No through road' and start climbing a steep hill,' commented one guest. High up in the Yorkshire Dales, surrounded by open meadows, with wide-open views across the valley, stands John and Barbara Drew's 17thC farmhouse. Rooms are cosy, with original beams, stone floors, even a massive press, once used to make Wensleydale cheese.

The Drews are experienced hosts, whose friendly but low-key welcome suits the quiet, restful setting. Barbara is a graphic artist, whose delightfully whimsical Christmas cards adorn the staircase. She also chose the pretty colour schemes in the bedrooms. Two look across the valley, a third faces the hillside. We particularly like this room, with its fruit-patterned wallpaper and claw-foot bathtub, but tall folk must be careful not to bump their heads on the low cross-beam. Meals are served at separate tables 'because that's what we prefer'. A chalk board in the dining-room displays the set menu, suggested wines and even the taped music, 'this evening by Schumann and Chopin'.

Nearby Hawes, Bolton Castle; walking.
Directions 11 miles W of Leyburn, off A684. Get directions.

Askrigg, Leyburn, North Yorkshire DL8 3JF	**Credit cards** MC, V
Tel and Fax (01969) 650443	**Children** over 10
Location on hillside deep in the country; ample car parking	**Disabled** not suitable
	Pets no
	Closed early Nov to early Jan
Evening meal by request	**Languages** some German
Prices £££	**Proprietors** John and Barbara Drew
Rooms 3 double; all have telephone, TV, radio, hairdrier, tea/coffee kit	
Facilities sitting-room, dining-room; garden	
Smoking outdoors only	

Yorkshire

Brafferton Hall

To city folk used to the hustle and bustle of urban life, the emptiness of deep countryside can come as a shock. Around Brafferton, fields are flat and open, while in the village itself, three of the four pubs were closed when our inspector passed through on a Tuesday lunchtime. Yet only ten minutes before, he had been driving in heavy traffic down the A1 motorway.

The hostess in this early-18thC Georgian mansion is Sue White, who manages to be 'charming and welcoming' and 'brisk and efficient', all at the same time. Her decoration epitomizes the genteel look seen in many upmarket bed-and-breakfasts. There are pelmets and tie-backs for curtains, plus shelves of books, antique furniture and ornaments. Unlike some grand homes, the whole of the house is free for guests to enjoy.

German and Spanish visitors told our inspector that they appreciated the 'Englishness of the ambience, the international dinner menus and, most of all, the traditional breakfast', which included home-baked bread and free-range eggs.

Nearby Yorkshire Moors and Dales, York.

Directions 20 miles NW of York. Take A59, then A1 north. Turn off at Boroughbridge. Get final directions.

Brafferton/Helperby, York YO6 2NZ
Tel and Fax (01423) 360352
Location on edge of quiet village; ample car parking
Evening meal by request
Prices £££
Rooms 3 double; 1 single; all have TV, radio, hairdrier, tea/coffee kit
Facilities 2 sitting-rooms, dining-room; garden, terrace
Smoking outdoors only
Credit cards AE, MC, V

Children welcome
Disabled not suitable
Pets by arrangement
Closed never
Languages French, German, Spanish
Proprietors Sue and John White

Yorkshire

Dacre, NW of Harrogate

Low Hall

There are many stone farmhouses in the Yorkshire Dales but Low Hall is special because of its atmosphere. The magnificent 350-year-old building comes with mullion windows and oak beams. In the sombre dining-room, the sense of the past is emphasized by the oak table and panelling; by contrast, the breakfast room is a cheerful yellow and blue. Although spotlessly clean and rich with character, there is a lived-in look to the rooms in Low Hall, so we do not recommend it for those with sophisticated tastes.

Don't be put off by the muddy farmyard at the end of the long driveway. Owner Mrs Holliday, with her cardigan and floppy everyday trousers, is a farmer first and a hostess second. Although she raises Aberdeen Angus cattle, she also enjoys meeting and cooking for guests from all over the world. The only rule is the minimum stay of two nights because, "if people stay just one night, you don't get to know them." Visitors from abroad are particularly impressed by the huge garden, with its paths and ponds, shrubs and lawns.

Nearby Yorkshire Dales, Ripley Castle, Nidderdale Museum.
Directions 10 miles NW of Harrogate. Get final directions.

Dacre, Nr Harrogate, North Yorkshire HG3 4AA
Tel (01423) 780230
Location secluded setting in own farmland; ample car parking
Evening meal by request
Prices £££
Rooms 2 double; 1 single; all have tea/coffee kit
Facilities 2 sitting-rooms, dining-room; garden, terrace, tennis court
Smoking restricted

Credit cards no
Children over 8
Disabled not suitable
Pets no
Closed never
Languages some French
Proprietor Mrs P Holliday

Yorkshire

Kettlewell, N of Skipton

High Fold

Traditionally, bed-and-breakfasts were in farmhouses and cottages. Nowadays, however, all sorts of buildings, from old rectories to grand mansions, are converted for guests. Set in the heart of the Yorkshire Dales National Park, High Fold, once a plain stone barn, has now been cleverly renovated by Tim Earnshaw and Robin Martin. 'Don't be put off by the rather austere exterior' warns our inspector, who praises the interior for its combination of rustic touches and creature comforts. Old beams and stone walls are offset by thick carpets, antiques and paintings of the surrounding countryside by a local artist.

Although the bedroom upstairs is the largest, with a lovely view of the valley and nearby hills, the two bedrooms on the ground floor are equally attractive. Moreover, their bathrooms were designed by an architect friend who is disabled. (The Lodge, a small, separate building, is also wheelchair-friendly, but is now for self-catering guests only.). Dinner is communal, with a set menu which includes local farmhouse cheeses. The tidy village of Kettlewell is popular with walkers.

Nearby Grassington, Malham, Bolton Abbey; Pennine Way.
Directions 15 miles N of Skipton on B6160. Get directions.

Kettlewell, Skipton, North Yorkshire BD23 5RJ
Tel (01756) 760390
Location on edge of village; ample car parking
Evening meal by request
Prices ££
Rooms 3 double; all have telephone, TV, radio, hairdrier, tea/coffee kit
Facilities sitting-room, dining-room; terrace, garden
Smoking restricted
Credit cards no

Children welcome
Disabled 2 rooms suitable
Pets no
Closed Jan, early Feb; end July, early Aug
Languages Spanish
Proprietors Tim Earnshaw, Robin Martin

Yorkshire

The Manor House

Look down the valley from the front door of this trim stone farmhouse and all that you see belongs to The Manor House. Although the Caygills farm more than 1,000 acres, the agricultural buildings and equipment are well away from the house, up a tiny lane past the early-19thC parish church, 'the third church on that site,' Mary Caygill told us. She is the epitome of a farmer's wife, with a cheerful welcome that puts first-time visitors at ease. Her breakfasts feature local bacon and sausages as well as her own preserves. Unlike some hosts, who set a specific time for serving breakfast, she is happy for guests to come down when they like. Similarly, the only notice in the bedrooms is a warning that the water is very hot.

Popular with walkers who can choose easy paths along the flat valley, or more rigorous hikes in the hills, this is a relaxing, comfortable place to stay, even though prices are on the high side. Mrs Caygill does not serve dinner but sends guests to Hetton, a village half a mile away. There, the Angel Inn is renowned for its inventive and notably well-priced menus.

Nearby Skipton, Bolton Abbey, Pennine Way; walking.
Directions 6 miles N of Skipton, off B6265. Get directions.

Rylstone, Skipton, North
Yorkshire BD23 6LH
Tel (01756) 730226
Location in peaceful valley;
ample car parking
Evening meal no
Prices £££
Rooms 3 double; all have
telephone, TV, radio,
hairdrier, tea/coffee kit, iron
Facilities sitting-room, dining-
room; garden
Smoking restricted
Credit cards no

Children not suitable
Disabled not suitable
Pets no
Closed never
Languages English only
Proprietors Mary and Jim
Caygill

Yorkshire

Studley Roger, SW of Ripon

Lawrence House

Lawrence House, right on the doorstep of Fountains Abbey, is in Studley Roger, a hamlet of some 30 homes. The house is a showcase for the talents of owner, Harriet Highley, a skilled interior designer. She has furnished this grand Georgian house with fine fabrics and intriguing paintings, which suit the well-proportioned rooms and spacious hallways. With two teenage boys in the family, however, there is no risk of the atmosphere becoming museum-like. As for the garden, this draws admiring experts and has been featured in magazines.

When it comes to breakfast, guests can order what they like, 'even black pudding,' but Mrs Highley finds that fewer want the full English breakfast nowadays. Perhaps her splendid four-course dinners are partly to blame. Prices here are high, but can be justified, particularly for a special occasion.

Fountains Abbey is not to be missed. The ruins of this 12thC Cistercian monastery are one of the most romantic sights in England. Adjoining the abbey grounds is Studley Royal, an Elizabethan mansion with a well-known water garden.

Nearby Fountains Abbey, Yorkshire Dales, Harrogate, York.
Directions 2 miles SW of Ripon. Get final directions.

Studley Roger, Ripon, North Yorkshire HG4 3AY
Tel (01765) 600947
Fax (01765) 609297
Location on edge of village; ample car parking
Evening meal by request
Prices ££££
Rooms 2 double; all have tea/coffee kit
Facilities sitting-room, dining-room; garden, terrace
Smoking restricted
Credit cards no

Children not suitable
Disabled not suitable
Pets by arrangement
Closed Christmas, New Year
Languages French
Proprietors John and Harriet Highley

Yorkshire

York

23 St Mary's

York is a year-round destination, with visitors coming from all over the world to admire the medieval Minster, tour the city walls and see the numerous museums. Since much of the heart of this compact city is closed to traffic, walking is a pleasure and the bed-and-breakfasts we have chosen (*see page 119 and 172*) are all within easy reach of all the major sights.

23 St Mary's is larger than many establishments in this book, with nine bedrooms, including a useful family room as well as two single rooms, a rarity these days. As in many mid-19thC terrace houses, stairs are steep and hallways narrow, but here, brass lamps, bold colours and cream-toned walls dispel any hint of Victorian gloominess. Details such as embroidered sheets and swathes of rich fabric for curtains add to the sense of deep comfort. Owner Greta Hudson has a hotel background, and the businesslike atmosphere suits guests, who have busy days, whether they are here for a holiday or for work. Few take time to relax in the sitting-room or admire the small, flower-filled back garden, though they do appreciate the quiet, side-street location.
Nearby York city sights.
Directions off Bootham, which becomes the A19 Thirsk Road.

23 St Mary's, Bootham, York YO3 7DD	**Credit cards** no
Tel (01904) 622738	**Children** welcome
Location on side street; some private car spaces, permits for street parking	**Disabled** not suitable
	Pets no
	Closed Christmas, New Year
Evening meal no	**Languages** English only
Prices ££–£££	**Proprietor** Greta Hudson
Rooms 6 double; 2 single; 1 family; all have telephone, TV, hairdrier, tea/coffee kit	
Facilities sitting-room, dining-room; garden	
Smoking restricted	

Yorkshire

York

Easton's

Built in 1878 as a wine merchant's house, Easton's has the marble fireplaces, decorative plasterwork and wood panelling that befitted a man of means. It was opened to guests in 1991 by Lynn Keir, who has since expanded into the house next door.

Now, she has a total of ten bedrooms, all decorated in an appropriate Victorian style. Aficionados of William Morris prints can spot the various designs used, such as 'Compton', a stylized tulip pattern in room 5. This is one of the most spacious, with two large windows under the eaves and an attractive mahogany bedhead. As in most old houses, bedrooms vary in size, as do bathrooms, which may be fitted into odd spaces. In room 1, for example, the shower is cupboard-sized. Although Easton's faces a main street, doubleglazing in front rooms should eliminate traffic noise. Breakfast is at separate tables.

Although this is not a 'family home' bed-and-breakfast, we give it a high rating for comfort and quality. From here, guests can walk by the River Ouse, through the park and over a bridge to the old city. Winter rates for the smaller rooms are a bargain.

Nearby York city sights, racecourse.

Directions Bishopthorpe Road is S of heart of city.

---

90 Bishopthorpe Road, York YO2 1JS
Tel (01904) 626646
Location on main road; some private car parking
Evening meal no
Prices £–£££
Rooms 10 double; 1 family; all have TV, radio, hairdrier, tea/coffee kit
Facilities sitting-room, dining-room
Smoking outdoors only
Credit cards no

Children over 5
Disabled not suitable
Pets no
Closed Christmas
Languages English only
Proprietor Lynn Keir

 ➡ *More on page 171*

The North-West

New Capernwray Farm

The Lake District, the Yorkshire Dales and the Forest of Bowland, a former royal hunting area, are all within a 20-minute drive of this wide open valley. Add in pretty villages such as Kirkby Lonsdale, Dent and even the hamlet of Capernwray itself, and this 300-year old whitewashed stone farmhouse becomes more than just a useful place to stop for the night. Although the farming days are long gone, views are completely rural, across peaceful meadows to rolling hills. Yet the M6 motorway is only a few minutes away.

Sally and Peter Townend have lived here for 25 years and are keen to promote the area. Asparagus, potatoes and soft fruits are from a nearby farm, whose strawberries "are so delicious, I put out a bowl at breakfast-time as well as using them in desserts". Nowadays, some bed-and-breakfasts are virtually small hotels, while others have furnishings straight out of design magazines. By contrast, New Capernwray Farm still retains its family atmosphere, with homely comforts. Bedrooms are decorated in easy-on-the-eye tones of peach, cream and pink.

Nearby Lancaster, bird-watching at Leighton Moss, walking.
Directions near Junction 35 of M6. Get final directions.

Capernwray, Carnforth, Lancashire LA6 1AD
Tel and Fax (01524) 734284
E-mail NewCapFarm@aol.com
Location in countryside; ample car parking
Evening meal by request
Prices £££
Rooms 3 double; all have TV, radio, hairdrier, tea/coffee kit
Facilities sitting-room, dining-room; garden
Smoking outdoors only

Credit cards MC, V
Children over 10
Disabled not suitable
Pets by arrangement
Closed Nov to end Feb
Languages English only
Proprietors Sally and Peter Townend

The North-West

Malpas

Laurel Farm

Anthea Few grew up in this peaceful countryside just a couple of miles from the Welsh border. After working in London, she returned to her roots, renovated this brick farmhouse and opened to guests in 1990. Although Laurel Farm is a handy base for sightseeing in nearby Chester or Shrewsbury, its proprietor is keen for guests to discover the less-publicized places even closer to hand. There are neatly kept, historic villages such as Overton and Malpas, plus gardens, abbeys, castles and stately homes.

Laurel Farm is hidden down a country lane. The house, originally two cottages, has been extended over the centuries but remains cosy rather than grand. Old quarry tiles on the floors, handsome antiques and an eclectic collection of china create a personal, homey look. Breakfast on the Regency dining table is a treat: on a summer morning, we had a compote of gooseberries, local ham and cheese, and delicious breads. Mrs Few is a professional caterer, so dinners (minimum of four guests) are of a high standard. Bedrooms are comfortable; two in the annexe share a sitting-room, one is on the ground floor.

Nearby Chester, Shrewsbury, Erddig; golf, walking, cycling.
Directions 1 mile W of Malpas. Get final directions.

Chorlton Lane, Malpas, Cheshire SY14 7ES
Tel and Fax (01948) 860291
Location in deep countryside; ample car parking
Evening meal by request
Prices £££
Rooms 4 double; all have telephone, TV, radio, hairdrier, tea/coffee kit
Facilities sitting-room, dining-room; garden
Smoking outdoors only
Credit cards no

Children over 12
Disabled not suitable
Pets no
Closed never
Languages French
Proprietor Anthea Few

The North-West

Tilston Lodge

'Yet another fine place to stay in the border country between England and Wales' was the reaction of our inspector to Tilston Lodge. Standing high on a hill, it was built as a hunting lodge in the mid-19thC and comes with stables and 16 acres of fields. The Ritchies raise Hebridean and Manx Loghtan sheep, rare breeds that date back to Celtic times. They also have white peacocks, whose feathers in a vase add an exotic touch to the high-ceilinged entrance. Some Victorian houses look rather gloomy; here, walls are painted white, so rooms are light and airy. A favourite bedroom is the spacious pine room, with its four-poster bed, 'a labour of love' that was made by a local carpenter.

In many bed-and-breakfasts, the guests' sitting-room turns out to be either small or formal; this is one where you can really make yourself at home. An enormous former billiard room, with a 10-foot-high ceiling, it has books to borrow and sofas to curl up in. Kathie Ritchie no longer offers dinner, but there is a pub in the village and restaurants nearby. On arrival, beware the sharp turning from the road into the driveway .

Nearby Chester, Shrewsbury; golf, walking, cycling.
Directions 3 miles N of Malpas. Get final directions.

Tilston, Malpas, Cheshire
SY14 7DR
Tel and Fax (01829) 250223
Location just outside village above country lane; ample car parking
Evening meal no
Prices £££
Rooms 3 double; all have TV, radio, hairdrier, tea/coffee kit
Facilities 2 sitting-rooms, dining-room; garden
Smoking outdoors only

Credit cards no
Children welcome
Disabled not suitable
Pets no
Closed never
Languages French, some Italian
Proprietors Kathie and Neil Ritchie

➡ *More on page 173*

The Lake District and The North

Rowanfield Country House

The Lake District, with its natural beauty and literary connections, draws visitors from all over the world. In high season, the main road through Ambleside is busy, tea shops are crowded and peace can be hard to find. One answer is to stay at this white-painted stone cottage set on a hill above and away from the bustle of the town. Apart from the view, the attractions here are the food and the hiking trails, starting right from the door. At the end of the day, walkers come back 'tired out and starving,' according to *chef patron* Philip Butcher, who used to run a restaurant in Windermere. He offers a choice of dishes at dinner, served at 7 pm in the jolly, flagstoned dining-room. The inventive menus could include fresh salmon with a lime and cumin hollandaise sauce or hot chocolate tart with a chocolate and brandy sauce. The homely, rather small sitting-room has a wood stove, while the eight bedrooms look fresh and uncluttered. First-time guests usually insist on having a room at the front, looking over the church spire to Windermere, but rooms at the back are larger and have mountain views.

Nearby Ambleside, Bridge House (National Trust); walking.
Directions 1 mile NE of Ambleside. Get final directions.

Kirkstone Road, Ambleside, Cumbria LA22 9ET
Tel (015394) 33686
Fax (015394) 31569
Location just outside town, on hillside; ample car parking
Evening meal by request
Prices £££
Rooms 8 double; all have TV, radio, hairdrier, tea/coffee kit
Facilities sitting-room, dining-room; garden
Smoking outdoors only

Credit cards MC, V
Children over 5
Disabled not suitable
Pets no
Closed Nov to mid-Dec; after New Year to Easter
Languages some French
Proprietors Jane and Philip Butcher

The Lake District and The North

Beadnell, N of Alnwick

Beach Court

Bed-and-breakfasts 'right on the beach' are few and far between, so we were delighted to find a house of this quality, right by the sea. Beach Court, a red-roofed house built of honey-coloured stone, overlooks Beadnell's tiny, photogenic harbour. 'The water is so close you can almost touch it,' according to one visitor, while the bedrooms boast 'some of the best views in the north-east, both over the bay and to the Cheviot Hills.' The Cheviot Suite, set in a corner turret, is the grandest, with a canopy bed that is emperor-, rather than king-size. As well as a sitting-room, it has the Crow's Nest on the top floor, which feels like an observatory, with views in all directions.

Former Londoners Carole and Russell Field are enthusiastic about Northumberland's empty beaches, sturdy fortresses and plentiful bird-life. Guests may borrow their boat, the *Peter Duck*, to explore the coast. Carole serves the freshest of fish. In fine weather, she barbecues on the terrace; otherwise, dinner is a candlelight affair. Verdict: highly recommended for a comfortable stay in a beautiful but little-visited part of England.

Nearby Holy Island, Bamburgh Castle; beaches, fishing.
Directions 20 miles N of Alnwick. Get final directions.

Harbour Road, Beadnell, Northumberland NE67 5BJ
Tel (01665) 720225
Fax (01665) 721499
E-mail russ@beachct.demon.co.uk
Location right on beach front; ample car parking
Evening meal by request
Prices £££–££££
Rooms 3 suites; all have TV, radio, hairdrier, tea/coffee kit
Facilities 2 sitting-rooms, dining-room, e-mail and fax;

beach-front terrace, garden
Smoking outdoors only
Credit cards MC, V
Children welcome
Disabled access to 1 room, special lift/elevator
Pets by arrangement
Closed never
Languages French, German
Proprietors Carole and Russell Field

The Lake District and The North

Brandlingill, W of Keswick

Low Hall

Enid Davies is the sort of cheerful, energetic woman who would make a delightful neighbour, if there were any houses nearby. Low Hall stands by itself in a broad valley on the quieter western edge of the Lake District National Park. "All I hear is the singing of birds and the occasional passing horse."

The house dates back some 300 years, but the outside shows little change from a photograph taken in 1891. 'It creaks, it slopes and so do we,' Enid says with a chuckle. Bedrooms are snug, with pretty floral prints. Downstairs, the large fireplaces, with their long lintels, are set into the original stone walls. As in most farmhouses of this age, both the sitting-room and dining-room are rather small, though there is space for a handsome burr walnut piano which guests are welcome to play. 'One man sat down and gave us a recital of Beethoven. It was an unexpected treat.' We like the relaxing, family ambience of Low Hall, which makes a fine base for hiking and touring, though some guests do as little as stroll along the river to Cockermouth, birthplace of William Wordsworth.

Nearby Keswick, lakes, fells; walking, golf.
Directions 10 miles W of Keswick. Get final directions.

Brandlingill, Nr
Cockermouth, Cumbria
CA13 0RE
Tel (01900) 826654
Location deep in countryside; ample car parking
Evening meal no
Prices ££–£££
Rooms 3 double; all have radio, tea/coffee kit
Facilities sitting-room, dining-room; garden
Smoking outdoors only
Credit cards MC, V

Children over 10
Disabled not suitable
Pets no
Closed Christmas, New Year
Languages French
Proprietors Enid and Hugh Davies

The Lake District and The North

Carlisle

Number Thirty One

Boasting 2,000 years of history, Carlisle dates back to Roman times, when it provided protection from the nearby Scots. Today, the town is often bypassed by visitors on their way to Scotland, but it makes an interesting and handy base for exploring Hadrian's Wall and the Lake District. Readers of our guides confirm that Number Thirty One is the best place to stay. The Parkers run a classic example of the new style of bed-and-breakfast, combining the luxury of a small hotel with the personal touches essential to a B&B. Never satisfied, they continue to improve their impressive Victorian town house, redecorating the bathrooms and the sitting-room and putting up ever more shelves for the wide range of books on the area. Choose from the quiet Blue Room at the back, the Green Room, with its decorative echoes of Japan, or the Yellow Room. This overlooks the front gardens and, on a clear day, you can see the Pennines. The outstanding food is the bonus. Philip is a self-taught chef, who receives praise for his home-smoked salmon and trout, homemade preserves, breads and even sausages.

Nearby Hadrian's Wall, the Lake District.
Directions in the heart of the town.

---

31 Howard Place, Carlisle
CA1 1HR
Tel and Fax (01228) 597080
E-mail BESTPEP@aol.com
Location on tree-lined street; limited car parking
Evening meal by request
Prices £££-££££
Rooms 3 double; all have TV, radio, hairdrier, tea/coffee kit
Facilities sitting-room, dining-room; small garden
Smoking outdoors only

Credit cards AE, DC, MC, V
Children not suitable
Disabled not suitable
Pets no
Closed Dec to Feb
Languages French, German
Proprietors Philip and Judith Parker

The Lake District and The North

Hazel Bank

"It was love at first sight," owner Glen Davies explains. "Even before we stepped inside, we had decided to buy the house." He and his wife, Brenda, were originally from the North of England and have holidayed in the Lake District all their lives. "We felt as if we were coming home." That was in August, 1998, right in the middle of the busy holiday season. Hazel Bank has a long list of regulars, who book 12 months in advance and stay for a week at a time. Most are walkers, who appreciate the packed lunches and the drying room for rainy days. Some guests, however, are fans of *Rogue Herries*. They come to stay in the house where early-20thC novelist, Sir Hugh Walpole set this family saga.

The Davies have made some changes to this small hotel: moving the dining-room and starting a refurbishment programme in the bedrooms. Ask for number 7, whose solid oak four-poster bed exemplifies their taste. The four-course dinners could include steak in red wine or salmon with wild mushrooms, plus interesting dishes for vegetarians. Traditional desserts, such as sticky ginger pudding, are a speciality.

Nearby Scafell Pike, Great Gable, Derwent Water, Buttermere.
Directions 6 miles S of Keswick. Get final directions.

Rosthwaite, Keswick, Cumbria CA12 5XB	**Smoking** outdoors only
Tel (017687) 77248	**Credit cards** MC, V
Fax (017687) 77373	**Children** over 12
Location on edge of village in valley; own car parking	**Disabled** not suitable
Evening meal yes	**Pets** by arrangement
Prices ££££ (for dinner, bed and breakfast)	**Closed** open all year
Rooms 8 double; 1 single; all have TV, hairdrier, tea/coffee kit	**Languages** some French, German
Facilities sitting-room, dining-room; terrace, garden	**Proprietors** Glen and Brenda Davies

The Lake District and The North

Selside, N of Kendal

Low Jock Scar

Some of the least spoiled walking country on the edge of the Lake District is just minutes away from this attractive home, set among trees, on the banks of a stream. As for the name, that refers to the path once used by Roman soldiers. The Midwinters were successful fruit farmers in the south of England before a career change in the early 1990s. Now they run one of the most praised bed-and-breakfasts in the area. Ready to advise guests on what to do and where to go, they like their guests to get the most out of their stay, according to one grateful holidaymaker.

The description of Philip as a 'mad keen gardener' is borne out by the grounds, while his wife, Alison, has a high reputation for her cooking. A light afternoon tea is offered to weary walkers, but room must be left for the bargain five-course dinner served in the conservatory at 7.45pm. You could have carrot, parsnip and ginger soup, a smoked salmon tart, chicken poached in cream and white wine, sticky toffee pudding ... and then cheese. Vegetarians are welcome to order ahead of time. Of the five plain but practical rooms, three have a private bath or shower.
Nearby Lake District, walking.
Directions 6 miles north of Kendal. Get final directions.

Selside, Kendal LA8 9LE
Tel and Fax (01539) 823259
Location deep in country-side; ample car parking
Evening meal by request
Prices ££-£££
Rooms 5 double; all have tea/coffee kit
Facilities sitting-room, dining-room; garden
Smoking outdoors only
Credit cards no
Children not suitable
Disabled not suitable

Pets yes
Closed Nov to mid-Mar
Languages English only
Proprietors Philip and Alison Midwinter

The Lake District and The North

Threlkeld, E of Keswick

Blease Farm

'There are thousands of footpaths in the Lake District, so getting away from people is easy, even in July and August,' according to John Knowles. He has a catalogue of 200 suggested walks and drives, 'routes with a pub, by the water, low level and high level'. Passionate about mountains, he has hiked all over Britain and trekked in the Himalayas. Not only is the library at Blease Farm full of books about climbing, but bedrooms are named after peaks. Everest is, of course, large, with a huge window and panoramic view. Although Makalu recalls the highest summit scaled by John, K2 is named after the room's sloping floor, rather than the world's second-highest mountain.

This is no simple mountain hut, however. Although their stone farmhouse stands high on the southern slopes of Blencathra, it is spacious, comfortable and furnished by Ruth using unusual patterns and rich, bold colours. We could spend all day here, sitting on the terrace and pondering the extensive views towards Thirlmere. No wonder the Knowles, who only opened in 1995, already have a loyal following.

Nearby Keswick, lakes; climbing, walking, golf.
Directions 3 miles E of Keswick. Get final directions.

Threlkeld, Nr Keswick, Cumbria CA12 4SF
Tel and Fax (017687) 79087
Location high on hillside; ample car parking
Evening meal by request
Prices ££
Rooms 3 double; all have TV, radio, hairdrier, tea/coffee kit
Facilities 2 sitting-rooms, dining-room; terrace, garden
Smoking outdoors only
Credit cards no

Children over 12
Disabled not suitable
Pets horses by arrangement
Closed never
Languages French
Proprietors John and Ruth Knowles

Southern Scotland

Aberdour, N of Edinburgh

Hawkcraig House

Getting to this former ferryman's cottage is a minor adventure, since the white-painted house is at the end of a narrow road, at the bottom of a steep cliff. The setting, however, makes the drive worthwhile. Right on the edge of the Firth of Forth, the view is due south across the water to Edinburgh and Inchcolm Island. A pair of binoculars stand ready in the sitting-room, to use at the modern picture window. There is nothing fancy about the decorations, which include a wooden butter churn and a huge bell from a Second World War airfield. Elma and Dougal Barrie are down-to-earth hosts, with a fine sense of humour. Elma is also an excellent cook with room for a few non-residents to dine on traditional Scottish dishes, using fresh fish and local meat.

This may not appeal to those requiring space and luxury. Even though the bathrooms are modern, the bedrooms are rather small. However, it is a treat to walk along the shore to Aberdour's flower-decked railway station and catch a train across the famous Forth Bridge to Princes Street station in the heart of Edinburgh.
Nearby Edinburgh, St Andrew's; golf, boat trips.
Directions Aberdour is on N shore of Firth of Forth. The house is difficult to find. Get final directions.

Hawkcraig Point, Aberdour, Fife KY3 0TZ
Tel (01383) 860335
Fax (0131) 3131464
Location on north shore of Firth of Forth; ample car parking
Evening meal by request
Prices ££
Rooms 2 double; all have TV, hairdrier
Facilities sitting-room, dining-room; garden
Smoking outdoors only

Credit cards no
Children over 12
Disabled not suitable
Pets no
Closed Nov to mid-Mar
Languages French
Proprietors Elma and Dougal Barrie

Central Scotland

Aboyne, W of Banchory

Arbor Lodge

With its castles and whisky distilleries, grand gardens and summer Highland Games, Royal Deeside is a popular holiday destination. Arbor Lodge is on the same road as Struan Hall *(see page 132)*, and the two bed-and-breakfasts refer guests to each other when fully booked. While the hospitality is just as warm in both homes, the look is totally different.

Arbor Lodge feels more American than Scottish, perhaps because the Buchans also have a house in Florida. They are builders and designed this house themselves, using brick rather than the traditional local stone. Everything is on a grand scale, but the decoration is a little impersonal. 'More Dallas than Deeside,' was the reaction of one visitor who, nevertheless, enjoyed the rare luxury of walk-in dressing-rooms and cavernous marble bathrooms with gold taps and American-style showers. Outside is a large patio leading to lawns and shrubbery beyond.

This is not the place for anyone wanting a taste of history and the traditional Scottish experience. It will suit those who want spacious rooms and the best in quality and comfort.

Nearby castle, distilleries, the Grampians; fishing, golf.
Directions 11 miles W of Banchory, close to village green.

Ballater Road, Aboyne,
Aberdeenshire AB34 5HY
Tel (013398) 86575
Fax (013398) 86951
Location in village; ample car parking
Evening meal no
Prices ££
Rooms 3 double; all have TV, radio, hairdrier, tea/coffee kit, trouser press
Facilities 2 sitting-rooms, dining-room; garden, terrace
Smoking restricted

Credit cards MC, V
Children over 12
Disabled not suitable
Pets no
Closed Nov to Mar
Languages English only
Proprietor Mrs Sheena Buchan

Central Scotland

Aboyne, W of Banchory

Struan Hall

Looking at the solid mass of grey stone that is Struan Hall, we could hardly believe that its original site was five miles away. The house dates back to the 1800s, but in 1904 it was dismantled, moved stone by stone and rebuilt here, across the street from Arbor Lodge *(see page 131)*. Set in 2 acres of grounds, with lawns and an Indian-style pavilion, a rockery and carp pool, Struan Hall makes a restful, comfortable base, whether guests are sight-seeing, fishing, walking or playing golf.

Phyllis and Michael Ingham are accomplished hosts who have decorated their home to suit the Victorian atmosphere. Tartan carpets harmonize with the pine staircase, while the dining-room, where a communal breakfast is served, has a massive Victorian sideboard. Tiffany-style lamps light the hall.

Upstairs, the Scottish theme continues. The bedrooms are named after castles and have pine bedheads carved with Scottish motifs. Bathrooms, however, are right up-to-date. The Inghams do not serve dinner but are happy to recommend several pubs and restaurants in the town.

Nearby castle, distilleries, the Grampians; fishing, golf.
Directions 11 miles W of Banchory, close to village green.

Ballater Road, Aboyne,
Aberdeenshire AB34 5HY
Tel and Fax (013398) 87241
E-mail struanhall@zetnet.co.uk
Location in village; ample car parking
Evening meal no
Prices ££
Rooms 3 double; 1 single; all have TV, radio, hairdrier, tea/coffee kit
Facilities sitting-room, dining-room; garden
Smoking restricted

Credit cards MC, V
Children over 7
Disabled not suitable
Pets no
Closed Nov to Mar
Languages French, German
Proprietors Phyllis and Michael Ingham

Central Scotland

Ballachulish House

Anyone wanting to immerse themselves in Scottish history should head straight for this 250-year-old country house, set in a valley with stunning views of Loch Linnhe and the nearby Morvern Hills. The present owners, John and Liz Grey, can tell you all about the chilling connections with the Glencoe Massacre (1692), as well as the Appin Murder (1752) that inspired Robert Louis Stevenson's novel, *Kidnapped.*

Despite its bloodthirsty past, however, Ballachulish House is a peaceful spot where good food, good wine and good company are the order of the day. Local lamb and venison, vegetables from the garden and shellfish from the loch are the basis for Liz's gourmet dinners. Since portions are ample, it is advisable to build up an appetite by walking, fishing or perhaps enjoying a game of badminton or croquet in the garden. After dinner, guests may retire to play billiards and smoke, "just like the good old days," according to one contented visitor. The bedrooms are vast, with space for chairs as well as large beds.

Nearby Glencoe, Ben Nevis, West Highland Way; fishing, golf.
Directions 13 miles S of Fort William. Take A82 to South Ballachulish. Get final directions.

Ballachulish, Argyll PA39 4JX
Tel (01855) 811266
Fax (01855) 811498
Location on hillside in own grounds; ample car parking
Evening meal by request
Prices ££–££££
Rooms 8 double; all have telephone, radio, hairdrier, tea/coffee kit
Facilities sitting-room, dining-room; garden, croquet, badminton
Smoking restricted

Credit cards MC, V
Children over 3
Disabled not suitable
Pets by arrangement
Closed Christmas and New Year
Languages French
Proprietors John and Liz Grey

Central Scotland

Arran Lodge

Callander, north of Glasgow, has long been a holiday resort and a base for exploring the Trossachs and Loch Katrine. In a country dominated by grey granite, Arran Lodge comes as a pleasant surprise. The smart, 150-year old, colonial-style bungalow, which stands on the banks of the River Leny, has a white wooden balustrade guarding its deep wrap-around veranda. Even more surprising is the plush interior, with its deep pile carpets, white leather furniture and oriental ornaments, which seem almost too luxurious, so far from the city.

Owner Robert Moore, once a TV producer with BBC Scotland, is the thoroughly professional host. An accomplished cook, he offers a breakfast menu which is more like a brunch: fish pie, smoked salmon with scrambled aeggs, even steaks. All guests have to do is order what they fancy the night before and appear next morning with an appetite. His wife, Pasqua Margarita, is half-Italian and half-Scottish; she is passionate about her home, which has glamorous four-poster beds in three of the bedrooms, and even more splendid bathrooms.

Nearby The Trossachs, Lochs Venacher, Achray and Katrine.
Directions Leny Road is on the western edge of town.

Leny Road, Callander,
Perthshire FK17 8AJ
Tel (01877) 330976
Location on river bank;
ample car parking
Evening meal no
Prices £££-££££
Rooms 4 double; all have TV,
radio, hairdrier, tea/coffee
kit
Facilities sitting-room, dining-
room; garden
Smoking outdoors only
Credit cards no

Children over 12
Disabled not suitable
Pets no
Closed mid-Nov to mid-Mar
Languages Spanish
Proprietors Robert and
Pasqua Margarita Moore

Central Scotland

Ards House

Although many Scots emigrate south to England, sometimes the flow runs the other way. John and Jean Bowman have never regretted their move from a hotel in Lancashire to this pretty Victorian villa with its uninterrupted views westward over the Firth of Lorn to the Morvern Hills. Sunsets are truly spectacular.

The house itself tends to ramble, as additions have been made over the years to the original cottage. However, despite their commercial background, the Bowmans have retained a snug atmosphere, and even leave a soft toy on each bed. Their food, which is all home-made and competitively priced, is the great attraction. When we visited, the four-course set menu began with a hearty salad of venison, followed by mushroom soup, pork with apples and, finally, a spiced rhubarb ice-cream dessert. Even the bread is home-baked.

We recommend their two night mini-breaks which include dinner, bed and breakfast and offer outstanding value for money. Although the Oban to Tyndrum road runs right in front of the house, traffic is rarely heavy enough to disturb the peace.

Nearby Falls of Lora, ferries to the Hebrides, the Highlands.
Directions 4 miles N of Oban. On A85. Get directions.

Connel, by Oban, Argyll
PA37 1PT
Tel (01631) 710255
Location overlooking water; ample car parking
Evening meal by request
Prices ££££ for DB&B
Rooms 7 double; all have radio, tea/coffee kit
Facilities sitting-room, dining-room; garden
Smoking outdoors only
Credit cards MC, V
Children not suitable

Disabled not suitable
Pets no
Closed mid-Nov to mid-Feb
Languages English only
Proprietors John and Jean Bowman

Southern Scotland

Drummond House

Edinburgh has two distinct historic districts: the medieval Old Town and the classical Georgian New Town. Staying at Drummond House gives an insight into life behind the elegant façades of a typically grand 1819 home in the New Town, complete with high, moulded ceilings, a pillared hallway and impressive cantilevered stone staircase.

Josephine and Alan Dougall admit to a 'moment of madness' that resulted in their opening up their town house to guests. Unlike some bed-and-breakfasts that are virtually small hotels, this remains a home, right down to the slightly faded elegance beloved of the British. Canopied beds feature in all the bedrooms, of which our favourite is the suite with a huge bathroom and free-standing bathtub. The Dougalls' attention to detail is impressive: even the style of the modern showers and WCs reflects the neoclassical architecture of the house. Overall, we decided that the high prices are fair; besides, we found the Dougalls to be decidedly agreeable hosts. The only drawback is that cars have to be parked on the street.

Nearby Edinburgh and its castle, museums, galleries.
Directions Drummond Place is just N of St Andrew Square.

17 Drummond Place,
Edinburgh EH3 6PL
Tel and Fax (0131) 557 9189
Location on elegant square;
public car parking
Evening meal no
Prices ££££
Rooms 4 double; all have
radio, hairdrier
Facilities sitting-room, dining-room
Smoking outdoors only
Credit cards MC, V
Children over 12

Disabled not suitable
Pets no
Closed Christmas
Languages French, Spanish
Proprietors Josephine and
Alan Dougall

Southern Scotland

Edinburgh

Newington Cottage

Some visitors to Edinburgh insist on staying right in the heart of the city, but we would be happy to stay in Newington Cottage, despite the 10-minute bus ride. Freda Mickel and her husband opened in 1996 and quickly established themselves among Edinburgh's upmarket bed-and-breakfasts. Their Regency villa was built in 1832 by Thomas Hamilton, who also designed the old Royal High School which has been earmarked as the new Scottish parliament building.

The house was derelict when the Mickels took over and they admit that the renovation was 'a labour of love'. They restored the elaborate mouldings and chose antiques and reproduction furniture to suit the period. The result is delightfully light and airy. Bedrooms are 'more like bed-sitting rooms, they are so spacious,' one guest told us, 'and the bathrooms are equally generous.' The garden and quiet setting are added advantages. Freda Mickel does not offer dinner, since most guests prefer to eat in the city. Although guests have to park their cars on the street, the meters are inexpensive.

Nearby Edinburgh and its castle, museums, galleries.
Directions Blacket Place is off Newington Road. .

---

15 Blacket Place, Edinburgh
EH9 1RG
Tel (0131) 668 1935
Fax (0131) 667 4644
E-mail fmickel@newcot.demon.co.uk
Location on quiet residential street; public car parking
Evening meal no
Prices ££££
Rooms 3 double; all have TV, radio, hairdrier, tea/coffee kit, CD player
Facilities sitting-room, dining-room; terrace, garden

Smoking outdoors only
Credit cards MC, V
Children not suitable
Disabled not suitable
Pets no
Closed Christmas, New Year
Languages English only
Proprietor Freda Mickel

Southern Scotland

Sibbet House

During the 12 years that Jim Sibbet and his French wife, Aurora, ran this 1809 sandstone townhouse, they built a high reputation. The Sibbets have now handed the day-to-day management over to Jens and Anita Steffen, whose strength is cooking, but who only put on dinner parties for groups of friends.

The house remains a 'special occasion' sort of place. Once ushered into the lavishly furnished ground floor, first impressions are of well-proportioned rooms, a splendid staircase and cupola roof light. What sets this apart is the use of bold colours, striking furniture and Russell Flint pictures of exotic Spanish dancers. It takes confidence to decorate a traditional house in this style, but the Sibbets are former interior decorators and their skill shows. With six bedrooms now, the atmosphere may be a little more commercial than before, but an American visitor told us the high prices are worth it for the 'great service and great decor'. Honeymooners book well in advance for The Blue Room, with its four-poster bed, but we preferred the sunny primrose of the Yellow Room or the Patio Suite in the basement.

Nearby castle, museums and galleries.

Directions Northumberland St is just N of Queen St Gardens.

26 Northumberland Street, Edinburgh EH3 6LS
Tel (0131) 556 1078
Fax (0131) 557 9445
E-mail sibbet.house@zetnet.co.uk
Location in residential area; own car parking
Evening meal by request
Prices ££££ (2 night minimum)
Rooms 6 double; all have telephone, TV, radio, hairdrier, tea/coffee kit
Facilities sitting-room, dining-room
Smoking outdoors only
Credit cards MC, V
Children not suitable
Disabled not suitable
Pets no
Closed never
Languages some French, German
Proprietors James and Aurora Sibbet
Housekeepers Jens and Anita Steffen

Central Scotland

Fort William

Crolinnhe

Fort William has long been the jumping-off point for visitors to the Western Highlands. Active types come to climb Ben Nevis, Britain's highest peak, though the Nevis Range Gondola is an easier way to the top. The Great Glen, with its chain of narrow lochs along a valley, cuts away to the northeast. A short walk from the middle of Fort William, Crolinnhe has been the home of Kenneth and Flora MacKenzie since 1982. They restored the Victorian house and are constantly redecorating in what is a 'smart', though perhaps slightly old-fashioned style. This obviously suits the regulars who come here for the outdoor activities such as fishing, golf and hiking.

No doubt the 'breakfast at 8.30 am' rule also suits them. Guests decide the night before what they want, which helps the hosts, since 'the full works' can be a feast of porridge, followed by fresh Mallaig kippers or even haggis. More modest eaters can opt for fresh fruit or scrambled eggs.

Set on a hillside, Crolinnhe has truly spectacular views over Loch Linnhe. We would stay here for that reason alone.

Nearby Ben Nevis, West Highland Museum; fishing, golf.
Directions Grange Road runs parallel to the loch.

Grange Road, Fort William, Inverness-shire PH33 6JF
Tel (01397) 702709
Location overlooking Loch Linnhe; ample car parking
Evening meal no
Prices £££
Rooms 3 double; all have TV, radio, hairdrier, tea/coffee kit
Facilities sitting-room, dining-room; terrace, garden
Smoking outdoors only
Credit cards no

Children over 12
Disabled not suitable
Pets no
Closed Nov to Mar
Languages English only
Proprietors Kenneth and Flora MacKenzie

Central Scotland

Fort William

The Grange

Rob Roy did not sleep here but actress Jessica Lange did, when she was making the film about the Scottish hero with Liam Neeson. Like all guests, she would have been offered tea and home-made shortbread on arrival, and found fresh flowers and a decanter of sherry in her room.

We like everything about this Victorian Gothic home, which stands on a hillside overlooking Loch Linnhe. Where so many century-old houses here are a dour grey granite, The Grange is painted white, accentuating the bay windows, gables and turret. Joan and John Campbell are yet another couple who have rescued and restored a ruin. Although they retained original details, such as the grand fireplace in the dining-room, complete with carvings of deer and hunting scenes, they did not overdo the Victorian look. All three rooms have views over the garden to the loch, but our favourite is the Turret Room, with its curved window seat. Mrs Campbell does not serve dinner, preferring to concentrate on breakfast, which is a communal affair. The couple are experts on day trips, both inland and to the Isle of Skye.
Nearby Ben Nevis, West Highland Museum; fishing, golf.
Directions Grange Road runs parallel to the loch.

Grange Road, Fort William,
Inverness-shire PH33 6JF
Tel (01397) 705516
Location overlooking Loch
Linnhe; ample car parking
Evening meal no
Prices £££
Rooms 3 double; all have TV,
hairdrier, tea/coffee kit
Facilities sitting-room, dining-
room; garden
Smoking outdoors only
Credit cards MC, V
Children not suitable

Disabled not suitable
Pets no
Closed Nov to Mar
Languages English only
Proprietors Joan and John
Campbell

Southern Scotland

Galashiels

Maplehurst Guest House

The Scottish Borders area is known for its castles, its abbeys and salmon fishing in the River Tweed. It also boasts a long tradition of woollen manufacturing, which continues in towns such as Galashiels, where cashmere and tartans are high on visitors' shopping lists. Back in 1907, a local mill owner commissioned the building of Maplehurst, a stone mansion near the heart of town.

'An architectural experience,' was our inspector's reaction to the wealth of original detail in the style of Charles Rennie Mackintosh, the late-Victorian Scottish architect who is now a cult figure. A lively tapestry frieze of lions, deer and huntsmen gallops round the sitting-room, while fine stained-glass windows illuminate the wood panelling. Owner Janice Richardson has chosen fabrics and furniture in keeping with the period and even the bathrooms blend modern demands with old-fashioned atmosphere. A favourite room is the Turret Suite, where guests can lie back in the bath and look out over the rolling hills.

Nearby Abbotsford, Melrose Abbey; fishing, golf.

Directions entering Galashiels from the south on the A7, the house is 200 yards north of the main roundabout, on the left.

42 Abbotsford Road, Galashiels TD1 3HP	**Children** welcome
Tel and Fax (01896) 754700	**Disabled** not suitable
Location in residential street; ample car parking	**Pets** no
Evening meal by request	**Closed** mid-Dec to mid-Jan
Prices ££	**Languages** English only
Rooms 3 double; all have TV, radio, hairdrier, tea/coffee kit	**Proprietor** Mrs Janice Richardson
Facilities sitting-room, dining-room; garden	
Smoking outdoors only	
Credit cards MC, V	

Southern Scotland

Innerleithen, W of Galashiels

The Ley

Innerleithen means 'joining of the waters,' and The Ley is set in the valley where Leithen Water flows down into the River Tweed. Anyone searching for seclusion plus natural beauty will be satisfied here. Even the driveway is lovely, passing through a golf course, over a white bridge and alongside magnificent rhododendrons. Built in 1861 by a Scot who became a railway magnate in America, the mansion has the antiques, paintings and prints we expect of a grand house. Willie and Doreen McVicar, a retired couple, make quiet and unassuming hosts, but her background as a professional caterer ensures that dinners and the Scottish breakfasts are special.

All this does not come cheaply, but we feel that the luxurious bedrooms and bathrooms, combined with the setting, justify the high prices. For a honeymoon or anniversary, the spacious circular turret room, with window seats and wide-open views, is hard to beat. There are fine walks from the door and nearby Traquair House, with its famous Bear Gates, is a must.

Nearby Traquair House, Mellerstain, Abbotsford; golf, fishing.
Directions 12 miles W of Galashiels. Take the A72 to Innerleithen, then the B709 N for Heriot. Get final directions.

Innerleithen, Peebles-shire EH44 6NL	**Disabled** not suitable
Tel and Fax (01896) 830240	**Pets** no
Location in secluded valley; ample car parking	**Closed** Oct to Mar
Evening meal by request	**Languages** English only
Prices ££££	**Proprietors** Doreen and Willie McVicar
Rooms 3 double; all have hairdrier, tea/coffee kit	
Facilities 2 sitting-rooms, dining-room; garden	
Smoking restricted	
Credit cards no	
Children not suitable	

Southern Scotland

Jedburgh

Hundalee House

Seeing the peaceful countryside around Jedburgh today, it is difficult to believe that this land has a history of violent confrontations between the Scots and English. Among the attractions are the Mary, Queen of Scots House, a ruined abbey, a museum dedicated to Victorian prison life and Ferniehirst Castle, the ancient seat of the Kerr family.

Not far away is Hundalee House. Set back in the hills, this 18thC limestone manor house has been home to the Whittakers for a decade. They created the fine large garden, putting in flowering shrubs, adding peacocks and digging a pond for koi carp. Inside, the taste is even more exotic, reflecting their time in Egypt. Egyptian motifs hang on the walls and Egyptian hounds guard the fireplace in the sitting-room, which has fine views of the Cheviot Hills to the south. Bedrooms may not be luxurious but one has a four-poster bed. Two others share a bathroom; these offer notable value and are useful for a family. Sheila Whittaker does not serve dinner, but her breakfasts are 'cooked and copious,' according to one teenage visitor.

Nearby Kelso, Dryburgh Abbey, Abbotsford; golf, fishing.
Directions 1 mile S of Jedburgh, on A68. Get directions.

Jedburgh, Roxburghshire TD8 6PA	**Children** over 10
Tel and Fax (01835) 863011	**Disabled** not suitable
Location set in own grounds; ample car parking	**Pets** no
Evening meal no	**Closed** Nov to Mar
Prices £	**Languages** English only
Rooms 5 double; all have TV, radio, hairdrier, tea/coffee kit	**Proprietors** Mr and Mrs Whittaker
Facilities sitting-room, dining-room; garden	
Smoking outdoors only	
Credit cards no	

Central Scotland

St Andrews

Kinkell

Quality accommodation is hard to find in or near the golfing paradise that is St Andrews. Close to the Old Course of the Royal and Ancient Golf Club, many bed-and-breakfasts do plenty of business with little or no effort, so it comes as a relief to find a comfortable home where the owners still take pride in offering traditional Scottish hospitality.

Part-Georgian and part-Victorian, Kinkell is a rambling house in a quiet setting of trees and fields running down to the shore. We like the cheerful informality of Sandy and Frippy Fyfe, frustrated restaurateurs who decided to offer bed-and-breakfast because they enjoy meeting guests from all over the world. In contrast to the rather grand dining-room, bedrooms here are somewhat conservative, with the subdued colours of many family houses. The light twin-bedded room facing south still displays china models and porcelain painted by the owners' daughter. It is a pity that the only views of the gusty North Sea are from the small double room facing east. The tennis court and croquet lawn are an enjoyable bonus in fine weather.

Nearby St Andrews and its golf, university, cathedral.
Directions Take A917 S for Crail. 2 miles on left. Signposted.

St Andrews, Fife
KY16 8PN
Tel (01334) 472003
Fax (01334) 475248
E-mail gt38@dial.pipex.com
Location in country, outside town; ample car parking
Evening meal by request
Prices £££
Rooms 3 double
Facilities sitting-room, dining-room; garden, tennis court, croquet lawn
Smoking restricted
Credit cards MC, V
Children welcome
Disabled not suitable
Pets by arrangement
Closed never
Languages English only
Proprietors Sandy and Frippy Fyfe

➡ More on page 179

London and The South-East

Brakes Coppice Farm

For anyone who wants to stay at a traditional working farm, the Ramsdens' comfortable home is ideal. Close to the site of the Battle of Hastings and with views to the English Channel.
Directions 7 miles NW of Hastings

■ Forewood Lane, Crowhurst, Battle, East Sussex TN33 0SJ
Tel and Fax (01424) 830347 **Evening meal** no **Prices** ££ **Rooms** 2 double; 1 single; all have telephone, TV, radio, hairdrier, tea/coffee kit **Smoking** no **Credit cards** MC, V **Children** over 12 **Pets** no **Closed** Christmas, New Year **Languages** English only

Kenwood

The Goddens have a spacious Victorian home with a swimming-pool and croquet lawns. Antiques and porcelain grace their downstairs rooms, where a grand piano has pride of place. Well-priced, comfortable bedrooms. Informal. Near harbour.
Directions 4 miles W of Chichester. Get final directions.

■ off A259 Coast Road, Bosham, West Sussex PO18 8PH **Tel** (01243) 572727 **Fax** (01243) 572738 **Evening meal** no **Prices** £££ **Rooms** 3 double; all have telephone, TV, radio, hairdrier, tea/coffee kit **Smoking** yes **Credit cards** no **Children** yes **Pets** no **Closed** never **Languages** some French, German

Hatpins

The name is a clue to the former career of owner Mary Waller, who designed hats and wedding dresses before opening this exuberant house with its antiques, swathes of curtains and puffy cushions. Most find it romantic, some rather too fussy. Sauna.
Directions 4 miles W of Chichester. Get final directions.

■ Bosham Lane, Bosham, Chichester, West Sussex PO18 8HG
Tel and Fax (01243) 572644 **Evening meal** no **Prices** ££ **Rooms** 2 double; 1 single; all have TV, radio, tea/coffee kit **Smoking** no **Credit cards** no **Children** over 5 **Pets** no **Closed** never **Languages** English only

Magnolia House

Ann Davies' large home is in a quiet residential street. The best rooms are well furnished, though cramped. We like the Garden Room, with its bigger bathroom and four-poster. Car parking.
Directions St Dunstan's Terrace in west of city. Get directions.

■ 36 St Dunstan's Terrace, Canterbury, Kent CT2 8AX **Tel and Fax** (01227) 765121 **Evening meal** no **Prices** £££–££££ **Rooms** 5 double; 1 single; all have TV, radio, hairdrier, tea/coffee kit **Smoking** restricted **Credit cards** AE, MC, V **Children** over 12 **Pets** no **Closed** never **Languages** English only

London and The South-East

Bolebroke Mill

The 1995 movie *Carrington* was filmed in and around Christine Cooper's converted clapboard corn mill with its beams and wooden floors. Two bedrooms in mill, three in the barn which has steep stairs up to romantic four-poster honeymoon suite. **Directions** 8 miles SW of Tunbridge Wells. Get final directions.

■ Edenbridge Road, Hartfield, East Sussex TN7 4JP **Tel and Fax** (01892) 770425 **Evening meal** no **Prices** £££ **Rooms** 5 double; all have TV, radio, hairdrier, tea/coffee kit **Smoking** no **Credit cards** AE, MC, V **Children** over 7 **Pets** no **Closed** Dec to Feb **Languages** English only

---

38 Killieser Avenue

Owner Winkle Haworth is a keen gardener so her attractive Victorian house in south London overlooks a fine urban garden complete with picturesque arbour and climbing roses. Near station for easy access to central London. Relaxed family home. **Directions** 3 minutes walk from Streatham Hill railway station.

■ 38 Killieser Avenue, London SW2 4NT **Tel** (0181) 671 4196 **Evening meal** yes **Prices** ££££ **Rooms** 1 double; 1 single **Smoking** no **Credit cards** no **Children** yes **Pets** no **Closed** never **Languages** French

---

Bedknobs

Gill Jenkins combined two terrace houses to make this cheerful guest house in south-east London. The Green Room, with its plain pine furniture, is the prettiest and quietest bedroom, overlooking the garden. Convenient for visitors coming from Channel ports. **Directions** near Dulwich Hospital. Get final directions.

■ 58 Glengarry Road, London SE22 8QD **Tel** (0181) 299 2004 **Fax** (0181) 693 5611 **Evening meal** no **Prices** £££ **Rooms** 4 double; 2 single; all have TV, hairdrier, tea/coffee kit **Smoking** no **Credit cards** MC, V **Children** yes **Pets** no **Closed** never **Languages** English only

---

Ossian House

The Ashmans live in a quiet north London street, a bus ride from the Underground. Since 1996, they have offered an Irish welcome, comfort and eclectic furnishings. Rooms are small, but constantly redecorated. Useful for those on a budget. **Directions** nearest Underground station is Finsbury Park.

■ 20 Ossian Road, London N4 4EA **Tel** (0181) 340 4331 **Fax** (0181) 342 8494 **Evening meal** no **Prices** ££-£££ **Rooms** 4 double; all have TV, tea/coffee kit **Smoking** no **Credit cards** no **Children** yes **Pets** no **Closed** never **Languages** some French

London and The South-East

Wellmeadow Lodge

On an undistinguished residential road in west London, the Hornaks' busy guest house manages to retain the atmosphere of a family home. Although comfortable, bedrooms are expensive. Just six stops on the Underground from Heathrow Airport.
Directions close to Boston Manor Underground station.

■ 24 Wellmeadow Road, London W7 2AL **Tel** (0181) 567 7294 **Fax** (0181) 566 3468 **Evening meal** yes **Prices** ££££ **Rooms** 9 double; 1 single; all have telephone, TV, radio, hairdrier, tea/coffee kit **Smoking** no **Credit cards** AE, MC, V **Children** over 12 **Pets** no **Closed** never **Languages** some French

Mizzards Farm

Deep in the countryside, this delightful 16thC stone and brick house has elegant gardens. The Francis family home is very English, and they offer kippers and kedgeree for breakfast. The best bedroom has a marble bathroom and four-poster bed. Covered swimming-pool.
Directions 4 miles E of Petersfield. Get final directions.

■ Rogate, Petersfield, Hampshire GU31 5HS **Tel** (01730) 821656 **Fax** (01730) 821655 **Evening meal** no **Prices** ££–£££ **Rooms** 3 double; all have TV, hairdrier, tea/coffee kit **Smoking** no **Credit cards** no **Children** over 8 **Pets** no **Closed** Christmas **Languages** French

Playden Cottage

On the outskirts of Rye, tucked into the hillside and overlooking a canal and the marshes beyond, Sheelagh Fox's home has all the nooks and crannies of a country cottage. Bedrooms have low ceilings and small shower rooms. Pleasant garden; car parking.
Directions 1 mile N of Rye on Appledore Road. Get directions.

■ Military Road, Rye, East Sussex TN31 7NY **Tel** (01797) 222234 **Evening meal** yes **Prices** ££–£££ **Rooms** 3 double; all have tea/coffee kit **Smoking** no **Credit cards** MC, V **Children** over 12 **Pets** no **Closed** never **Languages** English only

The Old Parsonage

This 13thC flint house stands next to the 12thC church in an unspoiled village. Climb spiral, stone staircases to The Hall or The Solar bedrooms, with modern bathrooms, as well as beams and medieval windows. Angela Woodhams does not offer dinner.
Directions 8 miles SE of Lewes. Get final directions.

■ West Dean, Alfriston, Nr Seaford, East Sussex BN25 4AL **Tel** (01323) 870432 **Evening meal** no **Prices** ££–£££ **Rooms** 3 double; all have tea/coffee kit **Smoking** no **Credit cards** no **Children** no **Pets** no **Closed** Christmas, New Year **Languages** English only

London and The South-East

Pankhurst

Susie and Tony Rowse are the cheerful hosts at this elegant 16thC house, with its spacious grounds, tennis court and heated outdoor swimming-pool. The bedrooms are luxurious. Close to Heathrow Airport, with easy access to London. Golf nearby.
Directions 5 miles W of Woking. Get final directions.

■ Bagshot Road, West End, Woking, Surrey GU24 9QR **Tel and Fax** (01276) 858149 **Evening meal** no **Prices** £££ **Rooms** 2 double; 1 single; all have TV, radio, hairdrier, tea/coffee kit **Smoking** no **Credit cards** no **Children** yes **Pets** no **Closed** Christmas, New Year **Languages** English only

Scott House

On the High Street, Scott House is two businesses in one: an antiques shop and a bed-and-breakfast. The Smiths, who admit that 'the largest room is small,' have a faithful following who buy antiques displayed in their rooms and praise the breakfasts.
Directions on main street of West Malling. Exit 4 off M20.

■ High Street, West Malling, Kent ME19 6QH **Tel** (01732) 841380 **Fax** (01732) 870025 **Evening meal** no **Prices** £££ **Rooms** 3 double; all have TV, radio, hairdrier, tea/coffee kit **Smoking** no **Credit cards** AE, MC, V **Children** no **Pets** no **Closed** Christmas **Languages** French

The Country House at Winchelsea

Very much a spot for couples in need of recharging their batteries, the Carmichaels' 300-year-old country home has elaborate bedrooms, a candlelit dining-room and a walled garden. Mary Carmichael serves an enterprising set menu.
Directions 3 miles W of Rye on A259. Get final directions.

■ Hastings Road, Winchelsea, East Sussex TN36 4AD **Tel** (01797) 226669 **Evening meal** yes **Prices** £££–££££ **Rooms** 3 double; all have telephone, TV, radio, hairdrier, tea/coffee kit **Smoking** restricted **Credit cards** MC, V **Children** no **Pets** no **Closed** Christmas **Languages** English only

Late entries

Shortly before we went to press, readers suggested the following places to stay. They have not been inspected. Further reports are welcome. See details on page 32.

Forge Cottage, Chilgrove, Chichester, West Sussex PO18 9HX (01243) 535333. Atmospheric cottage next to pub with excellent reputation. 5 rooms. ££££

Highfield House, 12 Dowanhill Road, London SE6 1HJ (0181) 698 8038. Opened in 1997. Award-winning gem in a London suburb. 3 rooms. £££

The South and Channel Islands

Manor Farm

A base for touring the Cotswolds and Bath, or just relaxing, this trim 17thC farmhouse is in a quiet village, complete with duck pond. The Lippiatt family, who run a 550-acre arable farm, are experienced hosts who offer well-decorated bedrooms.
Directions 12 miles NW of Chippenham. Get final directions.

■ Alderton, Near Chippenham, Wiltshire SN14 6NL
Tel and Fax (01666) 840271 **Evening meal** no **Prices** £££ **Rooms** 3 double; all have TV, tea/coffee kit **Smoking** no **Credit cards** no **Children** over 12 **Pets** no **Closed** never **Languages** French, German

Highfield House

Although Pauline and Ken Parsons' home is modern, we include it because it is a quiet spot, but within easy reach of activities such as riding and golf, as well as Broadlands and Winchester. Bedrooms are practical and comfortable. Guests can also enjoy the lovely, large garden.
Directions 3 miles NW of Romsey. Get directions.

■ Newtown Road, Awbridge, Romsey, Hampshire SO51 0GG
Tel (01794) 340727 **Fax** (01794) 341450 **Evening meal** yes **Prices** ££ **Rooms** 3 double; all have TV, radio, hairdrier, tea/coffee kit, trouser press **Smoking** no **Credit cards** no **Children** over 14 **Pets** no **Closed** never **Languages** English only

Springfield House

Guests return to the Singers' 17thC home to relax in the garden, play tennis on the grass court, then stroll round the lake to eat dinner at a local inn. 20thC intrusions such as television are banned from bedrooms. Close to Longleat stately home, golf.
Directions 2 miles S of Warminster. Get directions.

■ Crockerton, Near Warminster, Wiltshire BA12 8AU **Tel** (01985) 213696 **Evening meal** no **Prices** ££ **Rooms** 3 double **Smoking** no **Credit cards** no **Children** yes **Pets** no **Closed** never **Languages** English

Rudge House

In a country village, this comfortable 150-year-old mansion has a vast garden, croquet lawns and a tennis court. Most guests, however, use it as a base to explore as far as Windsor and Winchester. Sandra Tose is an excellent cook. Well priced.
Directions 3 miles NW of Farnham. Get final directions.

■ Itchel Lane, Crondall, Hampshire GU10 5PR **Tel** (01252) 850450 **Fax** (01252) 850829 **Evening meal** yes **Prices** £££ **Rooms** 4 double; all have TV, tea/coffee kit **Smoking** no **Credit cards** no **Children** over 12 **Pets** no **Closed** last 2 weeks Dec **Languages** French, Italian, Spanish

The South and Channel Islands

Guernsey

Midhurst House

Chef/patron Brian Goodenough and his wife, Jan, were hoteliers on the mainland before moving to the island two decades ago. Their restored Regency town house has plain but comfortable rooms; well-priced evening meals include traditional dishes.
Directions next to Candie Gardens, 5 minutes walk to town.

■ Candie Road, St Peter Port, Guernsey, Channel Islands GY1 1UP
Tel (01481) 724391 **Fax** (01481) 729451 **Evening meal** yes
Prices ££££ **Rooms** 8 double; all have telephone, TV, tea/coffee kit
Smoking no **Credit cards** MC, V **Children** over 8 **Pets** no **Closed** Nov
to Mar **Languages** some French

Jersey

Champ Colin

On the east side of Jersey, the friendly Buesnels' 1812 family home is ideal for exploring the island's 'green lanes'. Stylish bedrooms; massive granite fireplace in the breakfast room.
Directions St Saviour is NE of St Helier. Get directions.

■ Route du Champ Colin, St Saviour, Jersey, Channel Islands JE2 7UN
Tel (01534) 851877 **Fax** (01534) 854902 **Evening meal** no
Prices ££ **Rooms** 3 double; all have TV, tea/coffee kit **Smoking** no
Credit cards MC, V **Children** over 2 **Pets** no **Closed** Christmas
Languages French

Middle Winterslow, E of Salisbury

The Beadles

David and Anne Yuille-Baddeley are hard-working hosts, who offer conducted tours of local sights and a collect-and-deliver service to Gatwick or Heathrow airports. Their house is modern, rooms are well priced. Anne takes pride in her evening meals.
Directions 5 miles E of Salisbury, off A30. Get directions.

■ Middleton, Middle Winterslow, Salisbury, Wiltshire SP5 1QS **Tel and
Fax** (01980) 862922 **Evening meal** yes **Prices** ££ **Rooms** 3 double; all
have TV, radio, hairdrier, tea/coffee kit **Smoking** no **Credit cards** MC, V
Children over 12 **Pets** no **Closed** never **Languages** French, Italian

---

Nether Wallop, SW of Andover

The Great Barn

Agatha Christie set her 'Miss Marple' stories in Nether Wallop, one of a trio of charming villages near Stonehenge, Salisbury and Winchester. The Quaifes have converted a lofty 16thC barn, which now offers comfortable rooms at reasonable prices.
Directions 9 miles SW of Andover. Get directions.

■ Five Bells Lane, Nether Wallop, Stockbridge, Hampshire SO20 8EN
Tel (01264) 782142 **Evening meal** no **Prices** £ **Rooms** 2 double;
both have TV, tea/coffee kit **Smoking** no **Credit cards** no **Children** yes
Pets no **Closed** never **Languages** English only

The South and Channel Islands

Poland Mill

Although close to the M3, Janice Cole's large, 16thC house over-looks a river and is surrounded by fields. One guest room has a four-poster bed. Nearby, Odiham is a pretty village with restaurants and medieval stocks, ready for miscreants.
Directions 6 miles E of Basingstoke. Exit 5, M3. Get directions.
■ Odiham, Hampshire RG29 1JL **Tel and Fax** (01256) 702251 **Evening meal** no **Prices** £££ **Rooms** 3 double; all have TV, radio, hairdrier, tea/coffee kit **Smoking** no **Credit cards** no **Children** yes **Pets** no **Closed** never **Languages** some French

Marridge Hill

Judy Davies and her ex-naval-officer husband have an informal home above the Kennet Valley. The well-priced bedrooms are comfortable, though only one has its own bathroom. Central for touring, ideal for those on a budget.
Directions 7 miles NE of Marlborough. Get directions.
■ Ramsbury, Marlborough, Wiltshire SN8 2HG **Tel** (01672) 520237 **Fax** (01672) 520053 **Evening meal** no **Prices** ££ **Rooms** 3 double; 1 has TV, radio, tea/coffee kit **Smoking** no **Credit cards** MC, V **Children** over 5 **Pets** yes **Closed** never **Languages** some French, Spanish

Laurel Cottage

Windows peer out from under the thatch of Graham and Adrienne Francis' 16thC, flint and brick home. Open since 1987, it has maintained high standards. Right on the A345, but near The Ridgeway trail. Cycles for hire. Two night minimum.
Directions 3 miles N of Marlborough. Get directions.
■ Southend, Ogbourne St George, Marlborough, Wiltshire SN8 1SG **Tel** (01672) 841288 **Evening meal** no **Prices** ££ **Rooms** 3 double; all have telephone, TV, radio, hairdrier, tea/coffee kit **Smoking** no **Credit cards** no **Children** yes **Pets** no **Closed** Oct to Easter **Languages** French, some German

Rookwood Farm House

Opened in 1996, the Digbys' Victorian farmhouse is handy for racing at Newbury and popular with business executives. One bedroom in the main house, two in the converted coach house, where breakfast is served. Heated outdoor pool.
Directions 3 miles W of Newbury. Get directions.
■ Stockcross, Newbury, Berkshire RG20 8JX **Tel and Fax** (01488) 608 676 **Evening meal** yes **Prices** £££ **Rooms** 3 double; all have TV, radio, hairdrier, tea/coffee kit **Smoking** no **Credit cards** no **Children** over 8 **Pets** no **Closed** never **Languages** English only

The South and Channel Islands

Sturminster Newton, SW of Shaftesbury

Stourcastle Lodge

Jill Hookham-Bassett's dinners feature produce from the garden; Ken collects Victorian kitchen implements. Uncluttered bedrooms have brass beds and pine furniture; two have whirlpool baths. Handy for exploring the coast and Thomas Hardy country.

Directions 8 miles SW of Shaftesbury. Off Market Place.

■ Gough's Close, Sturminster Newton, Dorset DT10 1BU **Tel** (01258) 472320 **Fax** (01258) 473381 **Evening meal** yes **Prices** £££ **Rooms** 5 double; all have telephone, TV, radio, hairdrier, tea/coffee kit **Smoking** no **Credit cards** MC, V **Children** yes **Pets** no **Closed** never **Languages** English only

Late entries

Shortly before we went to press, readers suggested the following places to stay. They have not been inspected. Further reports are welcome. See details on page 32.

Fishers Farm, Ermin Street, Shefford Woodlands, Hungerford RG17 7AB (01488) 648466. Peaceful working farm, close to M4 motorway. Indoor pool. 3 rooms. £££.

Plantation Cottage, Mockbeggar, Ringwood, Hampshire BH24 3NQ (01425) 477443. Attractive old cottage with garden in New Forest. 2 rooms. ££.

The South-West

Badminton Villa

Of the many bed-and-breakfasts on this quiet street, we chose Sue and John Burton's semi-detached house. Bedrooms have pine furniture and cheerful colours; the room at the top offers the best view over the city. Garden behind. Own parking.
Directions 1 mile S of city in residential district. Get directions.

■ 10 Upper Oldfield Park, Bath BA2 3JZ **Tel** (01225) 426347
Fax (01225) 420393 **Evening meal** no **Prices** £££ **Rooms** 4 double; all have TV, radio, hairdrier, tea/coffee kit **Smoking** no **Credit cards** MC, V **Children** over 5 **Pets** no **Closed** Christmas, New Year **Languages** English only

Manor Farm

Fans of the BBC TV *Poldark* series will recognize this as Nampara, but in real life Methodist preacher John Wesley visited this 17thC granite cottage. Comfortable but not luxurious, Joyce Cargeeg's home is near village and cliffs.
Directions 7 miles NW of Penzance. Get final directions.

■ Botallack, St Just, Nr Penzance, Cornwall TR19 7QG **Tel** (01736) 788525 **Evening meal** no **Prices** ££ **Rooms** 3 double; all have TV **Smoking** restricted **Credit cards** no **Children** yes **Pets** no **Closed** Christmas **Languages** English only

Nancemellan

Set in beautiful, well-maintained gardens overlooking the Atlantic Ocean, this handsome Victorian home is filled with antiques but feels informal. The Ruffs serve breakfast family-style in the kitchen with its Aga range. Cliff walks from the door.
Directions 7 miles S of Bude. Take A39. Get final directions.

■ Crackington Haven, North Cornwall EX23 0NN **Tel and Fax** (01840) 230283 **Evening meal** yes **Prices** £££ **Rooms** 3 double; all have TV, tea/coffee kit **Smoking** no **Credit cards** no **Children** no **Pets** no **Closed** mid-Dec to mid-Jan **Languages** English only

Broadview Gardens

Broadview is an unusual 1920s colonial-style bungalow, where the Swanns have deliberately retained a cluttered Edwardian style that some may find rather too formal. Well-priced dinner served on Wedgwood china. Their garden is outstanding.
Directions awkward to find. Get final directions.

■ East Crewkerne, Crewkerne, Somerset TA18 7AG
Tel and Fax (01460) 73424 **Evening meal** yes **Prices** ££–£££ **Rooms** 3 double; all have TV, hairdrier, tea/coffee kit **Smoking** no **Credit cards** MC, V **Children** no **Pets** no **Closed** never **Languages** English only

The South-West

Dartmouth

Broome Court

On the outskirts of Dartmouth, this golden stone farmhouse is at the end of a rutted farm track but surrounded by steep, immaculate gardens. Guests will find a peaceful retreat, filled with pine furniture. Jan Bird serves a hearty breakfast in her oak-beamed kitchen.

Directions 1 mile W of Dartmouth. Get final directions.

■ Broomhill, Dartmouth, Devon TQ6 0LD **Tel** (01803) 834275 **Evening meal** no **Prices** £££ **Rooms** 3 double; all have TV, tea/coffee kit **Smoking** restricted **Credit cards** no **Children** yes **Pets** by arrangement **Closed** Christmas **Languages** English only

---

Exeter

2 Deanery Place

There could be no better place to stay in Exeter than in the shadow of the famous cathedral. One of the two luxury bedrooms in Heather Somers' 14thC home has a four-poster; both overlook the 12thC South Tower. Some private parking.

Directions in cathedral close, in heart of city.

■ 2 Deanery Place, Exeter, Devon EX1 1HU **Tel** (01392) 490081 **Fax** (01392) 490380 **Evening meal** no **Prices** ££ **Rooms** 2 double; 1 single; all have radio, tea and coffee kit; 2 have TV **Smoking** no **Credit cards** no **Children** over 10 **Pets** no **Closed** Christmas, New Year **Languages** English only

---

Frome

Stonewall Manor

An unexpected delight. In a huge garden behind high walls, this 16thC house looks like a Tudor film set, with atmospheric rooms and a fireplace that could hold a tree trunk. Eunice Hillman opened to guests in 1996. Great for history buffs.

Directions Difficult to find. Get directions.

■ Culver Hill, Frome, Somerset BA11 4AS **Tel** (01373) 462131 **Evening meal** no **Prices** ££ **Rooms** 4 double; all have tea/coffee kit **Smoking** no **Credit cards** no **Children** over 8 **Pets** no **Closed** never **Languages** English only

---

Horns Cross, SW of Bideford

Lower Waytown

Caroline and Chris May's 17thC thatched Devon longhouse is only half a mile from Barnstaple Bay. Bedrooms in the converted barn look modern rather than 'cottagey'; the round sitting-room is unusually spacious. Road can be busy in summer.

Directions 6 miles SW of Bideford. Get final directions.

■ Horns Cross, Bideford, Devon EX39 5DN **Tel and Fax** (01237) 451787 **Evening meal** no **Prices** ££ **Rooms** 3 double; all have TV, hairdrier, tea/coffee kit **Smoking** no **Credit cards** no **Children** over 12 **Pets** no **Closed** Christmas, New Year **Languages** English only

The South-West

Launceston

Hornacott

On the doorstep of Bodmin Moor, this 18thC stone house is in the secluded River Inny valley. The Otway-Ruthvens are keen gardeners, with just one guest bedroom. This has its own bright, modern sitting-room, so total privacy is guaranteed.
Directions 4 miles S of Launceston. Get final directions.

■ South Petherwin, Launceston, Cornwall PL15 7LH
Tel and Fax (01566) 782461 **Evening meal** yes **Prices** £££ **Rooms** 1 suite with TV **Smoking** no **Credit cards** no **Children** yes **Pets** no **Closed** Christmas, New Year **Languages** English only

Lydford-on-Fosse, SW of Shepton Mallet

Lydford House

James and Lynn Ribbons combine an antiques business and bed-and-breakfast in their large 19thC home. Right on the A37, this is a useful stopover rather than a hideaway, but rooms are prettily decorated, with hand-embroidered pillow cases.
Directions 10 miles SW of Shepton Mallet. Get directions.

■ Lydford-on-Fosse, Somerton, Somerset TA11 7BU **Tel** (01963) 240217 **Fax** (01963) 240413 **Evening meal** no **Prices** £££ **Rooms** 3 double; TV, tea/coffee kit **Smoking** yes **Credit cards** no **Children** yes **Pets** no **Closed** never **Languages** some French

Mylor Bridge, N of Falmouth

Penmere

This is one to watch. Since moving here in 1996, Sally and Richard Cuckson have been renovating their home. The bedrooms all overlook Mylor Creek, with its sailing boats at anchor. Large garden. Within walking distance of pubs.
Directions 3 miles N of Falmouth. Get final directions.

■ Rosehill, Mylor Bridge, Falmouth, Cornwall TR11 5LZ **Tel** (01326) 374470 **Fax** (01326) 378828 **Evening meal** no **Prices** ££-£££ **Rooms** 4 double, 2 single; all have TV, tea/coffee kit **Smoking** no **Credit cards** no **Children** yes **Pets** no **Closed** mid-Dec to mid-Jan **Languages** French

Norton St Philip, S of Bath

Monmouth Lodge

One of the oldest hostelries in the country is The George, in the heart of this photogenic village. Just up the hill is Leslie and Traudle Graham's comfortable home, where two of the bedrooms have doors on to the patio and garden. Quiet setting.
Directions 7 miles S of Bath. Take A36. Get final directions.

■ Norton St Philip, Bath BA3 6LH **Tel** (01373) 834 367 **Evening meal** no **Prices** £££ **Rooms** 3 double; all have TV, radio, tea/coffee kit **Smoking** no **Credit cards** MC, V **Children** over 5 **Pets** no **Closed** Christmas, New Year **Languages** German

The South-West

The Plaine

In 1996, the Whitwams took over the wisteria-clad, 16thC stone house, which has an 'olde worlde' dining-room and pretty bedrooms with four-poster beds. Riders and walkers may use the washing machine and drying room. On main street in village.
Directions 7 miles S of Bath. Take A36. Get final directions.

■ Norton St Philip, Bath BA3 6LE **Tel** (01373) 834723 **Fax** (01373) 834101 **Evening meal** no **Prices** ££–£££ **Rooms** 3 double; all have TV, radio, hairdrier, tea/coffee kit **Smoking** no **Credit cards** AE, MC, V **Children** yes **Pets** no **Closed** Christmas **Languages** some French, Spanish

---

The Old Rectory

Narrow lanes climb steeply up to this hilltop village. Jean Langton is an accomplished cook, whose guests visit Rosemoor Gardens, walk the cliffs and relax in the quiet garden. Bedrooms are pleasant, but this is a rather expensive experience.
Directions 6 miles SW of Bideford. Get final directions.

■ Parkham, Near Bideford, North Devon EX39 5PL **Tel** (01237) 451443 **Evening meal** yes **Prices** ££££ **Rooms** 3 double; all have TV, tea/coffee kit **Smoking** no **Credit cards** no **Children** over 12 **Pets** no **Closed** Christmas **Languages** some French

---

Irondale House

In a quiet village, opposite plain modern houses, this late-18thC home is a useful base for sightseeing in Bath. Guests relax in the walled garden, on the upstairs terrace, and in the spacious sitting-room. The Holders' two bedrooms are prettily decorated.
Directions 10 miles S of Bath. Get final directions.

■ 67 High Street, Rode, Bath BA3 6PB **Tel and Fax** (01373) 830730 **Evening meal** no **Prices** £££ **Rooms** 2 double; both have TV, hairdrier **Smoking** restricted **Credit cards** MC, V **Children** over 10 **Pets** no **Closed** New Year **Languages** some French, German

---

Somerton Court Country House

The turrets and castle-like frontage date from the 17thC but Pauline and Owen Stephens' home has 800 years of history. Bedrooms are comfortable, not luxurious, but are fairly priced. Opened to guests in 1997. A fun place to stay.
Directions 6 miles S of Glastonbury. Get final directions.

■ Somerton, Somerset TA11 7AH **Tel** (01458) 274694 **Evening meal** no **Prices** ££ **Rooms** 3 double; all have telephone, TV, tea/coffee kit **Smoking** no **Credit cards** MC, V **Children** yes **Pets** yes **Closed** Christmas **Languages** English only

The South-West

Riversdale

Maggie and Eddie Ellison are a jolly couple, who offer notable value for practical, comfortable rooms. At the end of the garden they have private salmon fishing on the River Torridge. This is the riverbank setting for the *Tarka the Otter* story.
Directions 5 miles SE of Bideford. Get final directions.

■ Weare Giffard, Riversdale, Bideford, Devon EX39 4QR **Tel** (01237) 423676 **Evening meal** no **Prices** ££ **Rooms** 2 double; all have TV, radio, hairdrier, tea/coffee kit **Smoking** no **Credit cards** MC, V **Children** yes **Pets** no **Closed** Christmas **Languages** some French

Infield House

Although standing just above a main road, this scores for comfort as well as convenience. Richard and Heather Betton-Foster took over in 1997. Our favourite is the cheerful room at the back, with its view over the garden to the Mendip Hills.
Directions Portway becomes the A371. Get directions.

■ 36 Portway, Wells, Somerset BA5 2BN **Tel** (01749) 670989 **Evening meal** no **Prices** ££ **Rooms** 3 double; all have TV, radio, hairdrier, tea/coffee kit **Smoking** no **Credit cards** MC, V **Children** no **Pets** no **Closed** never **Languages** French, some German

Bales Mead

Enthusiastic reports from readers have been confirmed. Peter Clover and Stephen Blue have made their Edwardian home into a luxurious retreat, overlooking Porlock Bay. Everything is stylish, from the decorations to the breakfast. Booking essential.
Directions 6 miles W of Minehead. Get final directions.

■ West Porlock, Somerset TA24 8NX **Tel** (01643) 862565 **Evening meal** no **Prices** £££ **Rooms** 3 double; all have TV, radio, hairdrier **Smoking** no **Credit cards** no **Children** no **Pets** no **Closed** Christmas, New **Languages** French

East Anglia and The East Midlands

The Maltings

Aldwincle is a peaceful, attractive village in an undiscovered area. Margaret Faulkner's award-winning 16thC stone farmhouse has lovely gardens and views over the fields. The two rooms in the separate Granary have their own sitting-room.
Directions 8 miles NE of Kettering. Get final directions.

■ Aldwincle, Kettering, Northamptonshire NN14 3EP **Tel** (01832) 720233 **Fax** (01832) 720326 **Evening meal** no **Prices** ££ **Rooms** 3 double; all have radio, hairdrier, tea/coffee kit **Smoking** no **Credit cards** MC, V **Children** over 10 **Pets** no **Closed** never **Languages** English only

Catton Old Hall

Bulging with oak beams and atmosphere, this attractive 17thC house is in a quiet suburb of Norwich. Business travellers and holidaymakers appreciate the Cawdrons' high quality: four-poster beds, power showers and well-prepared dinners.
Directions 2.5 miles N of Norwich. Get final directions.

■ Lodge Lane, Catton, Norwich, Norfolk NR6 7HG **Tel** (01603) 419379 **Fax** (01603) 400339 **Evening meal** yes **Prices** £££–££££ **Rooms** 4 double; all have telephone, TV, radio, hairdrier, tea/coffee kit, trouser press **Smoking** no **Credit cards** AE, DC, MC, V **Children** yes **Pets** no **Closed** never **Languages** English only

Church Farm

The Scotts' immaculately decorated house, full of beams, is in a small country village next to the church. Peter is a historian, who specializes in architecture; his wife, Maggie, is a first-rate cook, whose evening meals are well priced. Garden, tennis court.
Directions 8 miles W of Cambridge. Get final directions.

■ Gransden Road, Caxton, Cambridgeshire CB3 8PL **Tel** (01954) 719543 **Fax** (01954) 718999 **Evening meal** yes **Prices** £££ **Rooms** 3 double **Smoking** no **Credit cards** MC, V **Children** yes **Pets** no **Closed** never **Languages** English only

Cathedral House

When the Farndales restored this 150-year-old house, they carefully combined old and new, so attractive Victorian baths have modern plumbing. The large bedrooms face the quiet rear garden. Breakfast, at a farmhouse table, is communal. Parking.
Directions St Mary's Street is in heart of city, near cathedral.

■ 17 St Mary's Street, Ely, Cambridgeshire CB7 4ER **Tel** (01353) 662124 **Evening meal** no **Prices** ££–£££ **Rooms** 3 double; all have TV, hairdrier, tea/coffee kit **Smoking** no **Credit cards** no **Children** yes **Pets** no **Closed** never **Languages** English only

East Anglia and The East Midlands

Frating, SE of Colchester

Hockley Place

Set in 5 acres of orchards and meadows, with a heated outdoor swimming-pool and croquet lawn, Hockley Place is a luxurious retreat. Helen Bowles is a fine cook, serving well-priced dinners in the beamed dining-room. Spacious bedrooms.
Directions 5 miles SE of Colchester. Get final directions.

■ Rectory Road, Frating, Colchester, Essex CO7 7HG **Tel** (01206) 251703 **Fax** (01206) 251578 **Evening meal** yes **Prices** £££ **Rooms** 3 double; all have tea/coffee kit **Smoking** no **Credit cards** MC, V **Children** over 12 **Pets** by arrangement **Closed** Christmas and New Year **Languages** English only

---

Fressingfield, E of Diss

Chippenhall Hall

Deep in the Suffolk countryside, this beamed Tudor hall is well away from neighbours and noise. The Sargents offer the good life, with a dinner-party atmosphere and comfortable bedrooms. Heated outdoor swimming-pool.
Directions 8 miles E of Diss. Get final directions.

■ Fressingfield, Eye, Suffolk IP21 5TD **Tel** (01379) 588180 **Fax** (01379) 586272 **Evening meal** yes **Prices** £££ **Rooms** 5 double; all have radio, hairdrier, tea/coffee kit **Smoking** no **Credit cards** MC, V **Children** no **Pets** no **Closed** never **Languages** English only

---

Frostenden, NW of Southwold

Poplar Hall

Although this thatched 16thC house is set in a large garden in the country, the nearest beach, South Cove, is only 2 miles away. Anna and John Garwood can recommend walks and also nearby restaurants. Ideal for those travelling on a budget.
Directions 3 miles NW of Southwold. Get final directions.

■ Frostenden Corner, Frostenden, Nr Wangford, Suffolk NR34 7JA **Tel** (01502) 578549 **Evening meal** no **Prices** £ **Rooms** 2 double, 1 single; all have TV, tea/coffee kit **Smoking** no **Credit cards** no **Children** yes **Pets** no **Closed** never **Languages** English only

---

Gislingham, SW of Diss

The Old Guildhall

With its thatched roof, low-beamed ceilings and small windows, this 15thC house retains the 'olde worlde' atmosphere many expect in a sleepy East Anglian village. Ray and Ethel Tranter offer special off-season breaks. The local church is charming.
Directions 5 miles SW of Diss. Get final directions.

■ Mill Street, Gislingham, Eye, Suffolk IP23 8JT **Tel and Fax** (01379) 783361 **Evening meal** yes **Prices** £££ **Rooms** 4 double; all have TV, tea/coffee kit **Smoking** no **Credit cards** no **Children** yes **Pets** yes **Closed** never **Languages** English only

East Anglia and The East Midlands

Oakham

Lord Nelson's House

Overlooking the market square, with its butter cross and nearby 12thC Great Hall, this small restaurant with rooms makes a fine base for exploring England's smallest county. The best room is Lady Emma Hamilton's with its four-poster bed. Expensive.
Directions in corner of Market Place in heart of Oakham.

■ Market Place, Oakham, Rutland LE15 6DJ **Tel** (01572) 723199 **Evening meal** Fri, Sat **Prices** ££££ **Rooms** 4 double; all have telephone, TV, radio, tea/coffee kit **Smoking** no **Credit cards** MC, V **Children** yes **Pets** yes **Closed** never **Languages** English only

Spexhall, W of Southwold

St Peter's House

Hidden away in a quiet hamlet, Dr Judith Middleton-Stewart's 16thC tithe barn offers something completely different. Roof-beams soar high above the uncluttered drawing-room, with its grand piano and wood stove. Some rooms on ground level.
Directions 9 miles W of Southwold. Get final directions.

■ Spexhall, Halesworth, Suffolk IP19 0RQ **Tel** (01986) 873329 **Fax** (01986) 875275 **Evening meal** yes **Prices** ££ **Rooms** 3 double; all have radio, hairdrier, tea/coffee kit **Smoking** no **Credit cards** no **Children** no **Pets** yes **Closed** never **Languages** English only

Starston, NE of Diss

Starston Hall

The Baxters, who opened in 1996, have completely renovated their Elizabethan country house, with its original moat. The interior has admirable antiques and two sophisticated bedrooms. A third bedroom is in the Barn. Glamorous candlelit dinners.
Directions 10 miles NE of Diss. Get final directions.

■ Starston, Harleston, Norfolk IP20 9PU **Tel** (01379) 854252 **Fax** (01379) 852966 **Evening meal** yes **Prices** £££-££££ **Rooms** 3 double; all have TV, radio, hairdrier **Smoking** no **Credit cards** no **Children** over 12 **Pets** no **Closed** Christmas, New Year **Languages** French, German, Italian

Swaffham Bulbeck, NE of Cambridge

The Old Rectory

Naturalist Charles Darwin slept here 160 years ago. Now Jenny Few-Mackay is the enthusiastic hostess in an informal home full of paintings and furniture, with outdoor swimming-pool. Not the most luxurious house, but certainly a well-priced base for Cambridge and Ely.
Directions 5 miles NE of Cambridge. Get final directions.

■ Swaffham Bulbeck, Nr Cambridge, Cambridgeshire CB5 0LX **Tel** (01223) 811986 **Evening meal** no **Prices** £££ **Rooms** 3 double; all have TV, radio, tea/coffee kit **Smoking** no **Credit cards** no **Children** over 12 **Pets** yes **Closed** Christmas **Languages** English only

East Anglia and The East Midlands

Thaxted, SE of Saffron Walden

Piggot's Mill

Gillian Hingston's stylish conversion of a typical, clapboard Essex barn is in a quiet part of the old town of Thaxted. Breakfast is in the stone-paved dining-room, with its ancient beams. Comfortable bedrooms. Restaurants nearby.

Directions 8 miles SE of Saffron Walden.

■ Watling Lane, Thaxted, Dunmow, Essex CM6 2QY
Tel and Fax (01371) 830379 **Prices** ££ **Rooms** 2 double; all have TV, radio, tea/coffee kit **Smoking** no **Credit cards** no **Children** over 12 **Pets** no **Closed** Christmas, New Year **Languages** English only

---

Weston Underwood, NW of Derby

Park View Farm

Just outside the Peak District National Park and deep in the Derbyshire countryside. Linda Adams' comfortable Victorian home is named after its views over the National Trust property Kedleston Hall. A working farm. Pub nearby for dinner.

Directions 6 miles NW of Derby. Get final directions.

■ Weston Underwood, Ashbourne, Derbyshire DE6 4PE **Tel** (01335) 360352 **Evening meal** no **Prices** ££ **Rooms** 3 double; all have TV, tea/coffee kit **Smoking** no **Credit cards** no **Children** yes **Pets** no **Closed** Christmas **Languages** English only

---

Worlington, NE of Newmarket

Brambles

Well known to the horse-racing fraternity, Brambles is hidden behind high walls, with extensive gardens. Genny Jakobson's forte is cooking; husband 'Yak', a former racing journalist, offers tours to watch horses train at Newmarket.

Directions 8 miles NE of Newmarket. Get directions.

■ Mildenhall Road, Worlington, Bury St Edmunds, Suffolk IP28 8RY
Tel and Fax (01638) 713121 **Evening meal** yes **Prices** £££ **Rooms** 3 double; all have TV, tea/coffee kit **Smoking** no **Credit card** no **Children** yes **Pets** no **Closed** never **Languages** English only

The Cotswolds and The Midlands

Aylton, W of Ledbury

Priors Court

An idyllic spot in a fertile, peaceful valley, Judith Young's 400-year-old brick farmhouse stands reflected in its ancient mill pond. Inside are beams, an ancient chimney and a relaxing, family-home ambience. Ideal for walking, peace and quiet.
Directions 5 miles W of Ledbury. Get final directions.

■ Aylton, Ledbury, Herefordshire HR8 2QE **Tel** (01531) 670748
Fax (01531) 670860 **Evening meal** no **Prices** ££ **Rooms** 2 double; all
have TV, radio, hairdrier, tea/coffee kit **Smoking** restricted
Credit cards no **Children** yes **Pets** by special arrangement
Closed never **Languages** some French

Broadway

Cowley House

As well as welcoming guests into her 17thC stone house close to the village green, Mary Kemp still finds time to make jam using plums from the garden. Rooms vary: one has an Elizabethan-style four-poster bed, others are simpler but also comfortable.
Directions Church Street is off the main street.

■ Church Street, Broadway, Worcestershire WR12 7AE **Tel** (01386)
853262 **Evening meal** no **Prices** £££ **Rooms** 5 double; most have TV,
radio, hairdrier **Smoking** no **Credit cards** no **Children** over 3 **Pets** no
Closed Christmas **Languages** English only

Broadway

Tudor Cottage

Since 1996, Jane and Frank Allen have hosted visitors in their 17thC house on the main street. Bedrooms are freshly decorated in pretty colours; the breakfast room has leaded windows and old beams. Highly rated for its cosy cottage atmosphere.
Directions next to the Horse and Hounds pub.

■ High Street, Broadway, Worcestershire WR12 7DT **Tel** (01386)
852674 **Evening meal** no **Prices** ££-£££ **Rooms** 3 double; all have TV,
hairdrier, tea/coffee kit **Smoking** no **Credit cards** no **Children** yes
Pets yes **Closed** Christmas **Languages** some French, some Italian

---

Broadwell, N of Stow-on-the-Wold

College House

A tranquil hideaway in an undiscovered hamlet, Sybil Gisby's 17thC house has stone floors, exposed stone walls and even a priest's hole. Rooms are uncluttered, luxurious and stylishly decorated. She is a professional cook, so meals are special.
Directions 3 miles N of Stow-on-the-Wold. Get directions.

■ Chapel Street, Broadwell, Gloucestershire GL56 0TW **Tel** (01451)
832351 **Evening meal** yes **Prices** ££-£££ **Rooms** 3 double; all have
TV, tea/coffee kit **Smoking** restricted **Credit cards** no **Children** no **Pets**
no **Closed** Christmas, New Year **Languages** English only

The Cotswolds and The Midlands

Clapton-on-the-Hill, S of Stow-on-the-Wold

Clapton Manor

In another unspoiled Cotswold village, we found this historic 17thC manor house, next to a 12thC church. James Bolton is a professional garden designer; Karin is a fine cook and busy mother. Guest rooms, however, are in a separate wing.
Directions off A49. Difficult to find. Get final directions.

■ Clapton-on-the-Hill, Gloucestershire GL54 2LG **Tel** (01451) 810202 **Fax** (01451) 821804 **Evening meal** no **Prices** £££ **Rooms** 2 double; all have radio, tea/coffee kit **Smoking** no **Credit cards** MC, V **Children** yes **Pets** by arrangement **Closed** Christmas **Languages** French, some Italian

Kilcot, E of Ross-on-Wye

Orchard House

Anne Thompson lives in the countryside, within 30 minutes' drive of Hereford, Gloucester and Cheltenham. Her 300-year-old home is comfortable, with privacy in the stable annexe. Well-priced evening meal in Regency dining-room.
Directions 7 miles E of Ross-on-Wye. Get final directions.

■ Aston Ingham Road, Kilcot, Nr Newent, Gloucestershire GL18 1NP **Tel** (01989) 720417 **Fax** (01989) 720770 **Evening meal** yes **Prices** ££–£££ **Rooms** 4 double; all have radio, hairdrier, tea/coffee kit **Smoking** no **Credit cards** MC, V **Children** over 12 **Pets** no **Closed** never **Languages** English only

Ledbury

The Barn House

In the heart of this handsome market town is Judi and Richard Holland's historic home. Stairs with 19thC Chinese Chippendale screens lead to comfortable, though rather small bedrooms. Behind is the 17thC barn, used for parties.
Directions New Street is one-way. Get directions.

■ New Street, Ledbury, Herefordshire HR8 2DX **Tel** (01531) 632825 **Evening meal** no **Prices** ££ **Rooms** 3 double; all have TV, radio, tea/coffee kit **Smoking** no **Credit cards** MC, V **Children** over 15 **Pets** no **Closed** Christmas, New Year **Languages** some French

Ludlow

Number Twenty Eight

With a 900-year-old castle, plus Tudor and Georgian houses, Ludlow is worth exploring. Just below the medieval gate, Patricia and Philip Ross have comfortable, well-decorated rooms in three houses, with gardens, books, and open fireplaces.
Directions on S side of town, between archway and river.

■ 28 Lower Broad Street, Ludlow SY8 1PQ **Tel and Fax** (01584) 876996 **Evening meal** no **Prices** £££ **Rooms** 6 double; all have phone, TV, radio, hairdrier, tea/coffee kit **Smoking** no **Credit cards** MC, V **Children** over 12 **Pets** yes **Closed** never **Languages** English only

The Cotswolds and The Midlands

Pershore, SE of Worcester

The Barn

Pershore is between the Malvern Hills and the Cotswolds. In the grounds of her house, Gina Horton converted a 19thC barn into 3 comfortable bedrooms with exposed brick and beams. Use of tennis court and swimming-pool by arrangement. Well priced. **Directions** 8 miles SE of Worcester. Get directions.

■ Pensham Hill House, Pensham, Pershore, Worcestershire WR10 3HA **Tel** (01386) 555270 **Evening meal** no **Prices** ££–£££ **Rooms** 3 double; all have TV, tea/coffee kit **Smoking** no **Credit cards** no **Children** over 12 **Pets** no **Closed** never **Languages** English only

Shipton-under-Wychwood, NW of Oxford

Shipton Grange House

On the edge of the Cotswolds, Mrs Hill and her sister converted Georgian stables and a coach house into an attractive home with a well-tended walled garden. Restful colours in the sitting-room and bedrooms. Fair prices for real comfort. A peaceful spot. **Directions** 20 miles NW of Oxford. Get directions.

■ Shipton-under-Wychwood, Oxfordshire OX7 6DG **Tel** (01993) 831298 **Fax** (01993) 832082 **Evening meal** no **Prices** £££ **Rooms** 2 double; both have TV, tea/coffee kit **Smoking** no **Credit cards** no **Children** over 12 **Pets** no **Closed** Christmas, New Year **Languages** French

Tetbury, SE of Stroud

Tavern House

In an attractive stone hamlet near Tetbury, the Tremellens' house has a fine walled garden. Bedrooms are comfortable, if rather bland. Breakfast is at separate tables. No dinner offered, but pubs are nearby. Useful base for exploring the Cotswolds. **Directions** 10 miles SE of Stroud. Get directions.

■ Willesley, Nr Tetbury, Gloucestershire GL8 8QU **Tel** (01666) 880444 **Fax** (01666) 880254 **Evening meal** no **Prices** £££ **Rooms** 4 double; all have telephone, TV, radio, hairdrier, tea/coffee kit **Smoking** no **Credit cards** MC, V **Children** over 10 **Pets** no **Closed** never **Languages** some French

Towersey, SE of Thame

Upper Green Farm

In a hamlet between London and Oxford, the Aitkens have a fine 15thC thatched farmhouse with two bedrooms. Eight more are in the 18thC barn and former milking shed. Two rooms for disabled guests are a rare and welcome recent addition. **Directions** 2 miles SE of Thame. Get final directions.

■ Manor Road, Towersey, Oxfordshire OX9 3QR **Tel** (01844) 212496 **Fax** (01844) 260399 **Evening meal** no **Prices** ££–£££ **Rooms** 9 double; 1 single; all have TV, tea/coffee kit **Smoking** no **Credit cards** no **Children** over 14 **Pets** no **Closed** never **Languages** English

The Cotswolds and The Midlands

Winforton, NW of Hereford

Winforton Court

An enthusiastic reader recommends Jackie Kingdon's 16thC half-timbered mansion in a delightful village, deep in the country. The four-poster room has views over the well-tended garden to the Black Hills. Small library, large drawing-room with fireplace.

Directions 14 miles NW of Hereford on A 438.

■ Winforton, Herefordshire HR3 6EA **Tel** (01544) 328498
Evening meal no **Prices** £££ **Rooms** 3 double; all have radio, hairdrier, tea/coffee kit**Smoking** no **Credit cards** no **Children** yes **Pets** no **Closed** never **Languages** English only

Late entries

Shortly before we went to press, readers suggested the following places to stay. They have not been inspected. Further reports are welcome. See details on page 32.

Upper Buckton Farm, Leintwardine, Craven Arms, Herefordshire SY7 0JU (01547) 540634. Georgian farmhouse where owners are praised for food as well as comfort. 3 rooms. £££.

Wales

Hazeldene

Aberaeron is a popular seaside town, which retains much of its Georgian architecture. Jackie and John Lewis's grand villa, which dates from the turn-of-the-century, fills a need for comfortable and welcoming accommodation in the area.
Directions in town, easy to find.

■ South Road, Aberaeron SA46 0DP **Tel** (01545) 570652 **Fax** (01545) 571012 Evening meal yes **Prices** ££ **Rooms** 3 double; all have TV, radio, hairdrier, tea/coffee kit **Smoking** no **Credit cards** MC, V **Children** no **Pets** no **Closed** mid-Oct to Easter **Languages** Welsh

---

Abercelyn

Beck Cunningham organizes walking tours of Snowdonia; Judy runs the handsome 18thC house they restored after moving here in 1991. Just off the main road, in season it could feel busy, though the lake views are compensation. Excellent value.
Directions 1 mile SW of Bala. Get final directions.

■ Llanycil, Bala, Gwynedd LL23 7YF **Tel** (01678) 521109 **Fax** (01678) 520556 **Evening meal** yes **Prices** ££ **Rooms** 3 double; all have tea/coffee kit **Smoking** no **Credit cards** MC, V **Children** yes **Pets** no **Closed** Christmas **Languages** German

---

Plas Cichle

Not far from Beaumaris Castle, this hilltop house has views over the Menai Straits to Snowdonia. Mrs Roberts has an eye for detail, putting bottled water and flowers in the pretty bedrooms. Children enjoy feeding lambs on the working farm.
Directions 1.5 miles NE of Beaumaris. Get directions.

■ Beaumaris, Anglesey, Gwynedd LL58 8PS **Tel** (01248) 810488 **Evening meal** no **Prices** ££ **Rooms** 3 double; all have TV, radio, hairdrier, tea/coffee kit **Smoking** no **Credit cards** MC, V **Children** over 3 **Pets** no **Closed** Dec to mid-Feb **Languages** Welsh

---

Lancych

In a lovely, undiscovered valley, the Jones-Lloyds opened up their huge white Regency home late in 1996. Breakfast in the vast dining-room is a treat, with views down to the River Cych, where guests can fish for brown trout. High quality throughout.
Directions 8 miles SE of Cardigan. Get final directions.

■ Boncath, Pembrokeshire SA37 0LJ **Tel** (01239) 698378 **Fax** (01239) 698686 **Evening meal** no **Prices** ££££ **Rooms** 3 double; all have TV, radio, hairdrier, tea/coffee kit **Smoking** no **Credit cards** MC, V **Children** no **Pets** yes **Closed** Dec to Feb **Languages** French; some Italian, Spanish

Wales

Brecon

11 The Watton

After travelling the world in the British army, the Wisemans settled in this terraced cottage in the heart of town. Both are keen golfers and informality is the rule in their home. Rooms are small but decorated with flair and offer notable value. A find.
Directions The Watton is SE of middle of town.

■ 11 The Watton, Brecon, Powys LD3 7ED **Tel** (01874) 625650
Evening meal no **Prices** £ **Rooms** 2 double; 2 single
Smoking restricted **Credit cards** no **Children** yes **Pets** no
Closed Christmas and New Year **Languages** Welsh

Brecon

County House

Like much of Brecon, houses in this street are regaining their Georgian charm. Painter Robert Cope and his wife, Marylyn, restored this former judge's residence in 1996 with considerable style. The best bedroom is number 1. Own car parking.
Directions The Struet is a continuation of High Street.

■ The Struet, Brecon, Powys LD3 7LS **Tel and Fax** (01874) 625844
Evening meal yes **Prices** ££ **Rooms** 3 double; all have TV, hairdrier, tea/coffee kit **Smoking** yes **Credit cards** no **Children** yes **Pets** yes
Closed never **Languages** some French, German

Capel Dewi, E of Carmarthen

Capel Dewi Uchaf Farm

Fredena Burns' 500-year-old farmhouse boasts a carved oak staircase and medieval-looking dining-room where guests tuck into freshly baked Welsh cakes at breakfast. Bedrooms are attractive; the sitting-room is a little worn. Private fishing on River Towy.
Directions 4 miles E of Carmarthen, off B4300.

■ Capel Dewi Road, Capel Dewi, Carmarthen SA32 8AY **Tel** (01267) 290799 **Fax** (01267) 290003 **Evening meal** yes **Prices** ££
Rooms 3 double; all have TV, radio, tea/coffee kit **Smoking** no
Credit cards no **Children** no **Pets** no **Closed** Christmas, New Year
Languages English only

Cardiff

The Town House

Charles and Paula Mullins have taken over from the Zuziks, but American pancakes are still served at breakfast. The neat Victorian house has plain, practical bedrooms. Own parking; ten minute walk to Cardiff Castle.
Directions Cathedral Road is in the middle of Cardiff.

■ 70 Cathedral Road, Cardiff CF1 9LL **Tel** (01222) 239399
Fax (01222) 223214 **Evening meal** no **Prices** ££–£££ **Rooms** 6 double, 3 single; all have telephone, TV, radio, tea/coffee kit **Smoking** no **Credit cards** MC, V **Children** over 12 **Pets** by arrangement
Closed never **Languages** English only

Wales

Llanerch Vineyard

Want to try some Welsh wine? Peter and Diana Andrews produce Wales' only estate-bottled wine on a large vineyard outside Cardiff. A bustling business, with a café and tasting room. Bedrooms in converted farmhouse have simple comforts.
Directions 8 miles W of Cardiff. Get final directions.

■ Hensol, Pendoylan, Vale of Glamorgan CF72 8JU **Tel** (01443) 225877 **Fax** (01443) 225546 **Evening meal** no **Prices** ££ **Rooms** 4 double; all have TV, radio, tea/coffee kit **Smoking** no **Credit cards** MC, V **Children** over 3 **Pets** no **Closed** never **Languages** some German

Llwyndu Farmhouse

Food is Peter Thompson's passion but his mainly modern menus contrast with the medieval beams, low ceilings and circular stone staircase dating from the 16thC. Two four-poster beds in the main house; additional rooms in Barn and Granary.
Directions 2 miles N of Barmouth. Get final directions.

■ Llanaber, Barmouth, Gwynedd LL42 1RR **Tel** (01341) 280144 **Fax** (01341) 281236 **E-mail** PeteThompson@btinternet.com **Evening meal** yes **Prices** ££–£££ **Rooms** 7 double; all have TV, radio, tea/coffee kit **Smoking** no **Credit cards** no **Children** yes **Pets** yes **Closed** never **Languages** Welsh

Brynhir Farm

Ceinwen Nixon is a stylish farmer's wife who has welcomed guests since 1972 to this working sheep and cattle farm. The 400-year old dining-room is full of atmosphere; bedrooms have been upgraded recently. Regulars love it.
Directions 1 mile S of Llandrindod Wells. Get final directions.

■ Chapel Road, Howey, Llandrindod Wells, Powys LD1 5PB **Tel** (01597) 822425 **Evening meal** yes **Prices** £-££ **Rooms** 3 double; all have TV, radio, tea/coffee kit **Smoking** no **Credit cards** no **Children** yes **Pets** yes **Closed** Nov to Easter (open Christmas, New Year) **Languages** English only

Berllan Bach

Berllan Bach means 'little orchard'. Set in a lovely valley west of the Clwydian Range of hills, Bre Quinn's restored cottage looks half-sunk into the garden. Rooms are small but comfortable. Guests go hiking, riding, fishing and play golf. Very hard to find.
Directions 4 miles E of Denbigh. Get final directions.

■ Ffordd Las, Llandyrnog, Vale of Clwyd LL16 4LR **Tel and Fax** (01824) 790732 **Mobile** (0378) 835253 **Evening meal** yes **Prices** ££ **Rooms** 3 double; all have TV, tea/coffee kit **Smoking** yes **Credit cards** no **Children** yes **Pets** yes **Closed** never **Languages** English only

Wales

Llanstephan, NE of Brecon

The Old Vicarage

In 1997, dental surgeon Tony Thomas and his wife, Carol, opened their large gabled Victorian home to guests. The Blue Room has an antique carved French bed, the Red Room was the vicar's robing room. On a hillside, looking over the River Wye.
Directions 10 miles NE of Brecon. Call for final directions.

■ Llanstephan, Llyswen, Brecon, Powys LD3 0YR **Tel and Fax** (01982) 560373 **Evening meal** no **Prices** ££ **Rooms** 2 double; all have TV, radio, hairdrier, tea/coffee kit **Smoking** no **Credit cards** no **Children** over 12 **Disabled** no **Pets** no **Closed** Nov to end Mar **Languages** English only

---

Mold

Tower

History buffs book into the rooms in the medieval tower of the only remaining fortified house on the England-Wales border. Grand and full of antiques, this has been the Wynne-Eytons' family home for 500 years. Set in extensive parkland.
Directions 2 miles S of Mold. Get final directions.

■ Nercwys, Mold, Clwyd CH7 4ED **Tel and Fax** (01352) 700220 **Evening meal** no **Prices** £££ **Rooms** 3 double; all have TV, hairdrier, tea/coffee kit **Smoking** restricted **Credit cards** AE, MC, V **Children** not suitable **Pets** no **Closed** Christmas, New Year **Languages** English only

---

Montgomery

Little Brompton Farm

A few miles east of Montgomery and its ruined castle, the Brights run a working farm. Although quite small, bedrooms in the 17thC, white-painted house are stylish and comfortable. Separate tables for dinner. Well-priced meals and rooms.
Directions 2 miles SE of Montgomery on B4385.

■ Montgomery, Powys SY15 6HY **Tel** (01686) 668371 **Evening meal** yes **Prices** £ **Rooms** 3 double; all have TV, tea/coffee kit **Smoking** no **Credit cards** no **Children** yes **Pets** yes **Closed** never **Languages** English only

---

Rhostryfan, S of Caernarfon

Hafoty

The Davies' restored 17thC farmhouse boasts views of Caernarfon castle, Anglesey and even Ireland on the clearest days. Rooms in the main house are small; those in the converted stable larger. All are well furnished. Snowdonia is just a 20-minute drive away.
Directions 3 miles S of Caernarfon. Get final directions.

■ Rhostryfan, Caernarfon, Gwynedd LL54 7PH **Tel** (01286) 830144 **Evening meal** yes, except Mon **Prices** ££ **Rooms** 4 double; all have TV, radio, tea/coffee kit **Smoking** yes **Credit cards** MC, V **Children** yes **Pets** no **Closed** Dec, Jan **Languages** Welsh

Wales

Ruthin
Eyarth Station

Don't worry about the trains, the last one came through this former railway station in 1964. Cheerful hosts Jen and Bert Spencer transformed the platform, track and ticket office into a home with views across the valley. Outdoor swimming-pool.
Directions 1.5 miles S of Ruthin. Get final directions.

■ Llanfair D C, Ruthin, Denbighshire LL15 2EE **Tel** (01824) 703643 **Fax** (01824) 707464 **Evening meal** yes **Prices** ££ **Rooms** 6 double; all have tea/coffee kit **Smoking** restricted **Credit cards** MC, V **Children** yes **Pets** by arrangement **Closed** Nov **Languages** English only

---

Spittal, N of Haverfordwest
Lower Haythog Farm

Nesta Thomas wins awards for her imaginative cooking. Meals of home-made soups and pâtés plus lamb, salmon and traditional British desserts are a bargain. Bedrooms are small and unpretentious. Family atmosphere on a working dairy farm.
Directions 5 miles N of Haverfordwest. Get final directions.

■ Spittal, Haverfordwest, Pembrokeshire SA62 5QL **Tel and Fax** (01437) 731279 **Evening meal** yes **Prices** £–££ **Rooms** 3 double; all have TV, hairdrier, tea/coffee kit **Smoking** restricted **Credit cards** no **Children** yes **Pets** by arrangement **Closed** never **Languages** some French

---

Late entries

Shortly before we went to press, readers suggested the following places to stay. They have not been inspected. Further reports are welcome. See details on page 32.

North Wales

Delfryn (The Old Rectory), Betws Gwerfil Goch, Corwen, LL21 9PV (01490) 460387. Converted village rectory in countryside. Home cooking. 3 rooms. £££

Fron Deg, Abbey Road, Llangollen LL20 8EF (01978) 860126. Stylish mansion on banks of canal. 4 rooms. £££

The Old Rectory, Boduan, Nefyn LL53 6DT (01758) 721519. Antiques, fine gardens, edge of village. 4 rooms. £££.

South Wales

Glangrwyney Court, Glangrwyney, Crickhowell NP8 1ES (01873) 811288. Grand Georgian mansion in Brecon Beacons National Park. 4 rooms. £££.

Trewalter, Llangorse, Brecon LD3 0PS (01874) 658442. A country retreat in a tastefully converted farmhouse. 3 rooms. £££

West Usk Lighthouse, St Brides Wentlooge, Newport NP1 9SF (01633) 810126. Converted 19thC lighthouse. Eccentric and exotic. 4 rooms. £££-££££.

Yorkshire

Aldfield, SW of Ripon

Bay Tree Farm

Away from the working part of their farm near Fountains Abbey, the Leemings have converted a 17thC stone barn into six reasonably priced, plain but practical bedrooms, all with their own bathrooms. Useful for families on a budget. Hearty dinners.
Directions 3 miles SW of Ripon. Get final directions.

■ Aldfield, Near Fountains Abbey, Ripon, Yorkshire HG4 3BE
Tel (01765) 620394 **Evening meal** yes **Prices** ££ **Rooms** 6 double; all have TV, radio, tea/coffee kit **Smoking** no **Credit cards** no **Children** yes **Pets** no **Closed** never **Languages** English only

---

Easingwold, N of York

The Old Vicarage

This red-brick, Georgian market town is an undiscovered gem. Right on the main square is Christine and John Kirman's comfortable 18thC home. He is a trained pianist who sometimes plays the grand piano in the sitting-room. Walled garden.
Directions 14 miles N of York. Take A19. Get final directions.

■ Market Place, Easingwold, North Yorkshire YO6 3AL **Tel** (01347) 821015 **Fax** (01347) 823465 **Evening meal** no **Prices** ££–£££ **Rooms** 4 double; TV, radio, hairdrier, tea/coffee kit **Smoking** no **Credit cards** no **Children** over 13 **Pets** no **Closed** Dec, Jan **Languages** English only

---

Richmond

Millgate House

As well as its castle and cobblestones, Richmond has Austin Lynch and Tim Culkin's handsome Georgian town house. Rooms are luxurious with large beds and linen sheets. The walled garden wins awards and overlooks the River Swale. Restaurants nearby.
Directions off Market Place. Get final directions.

■ Millgate, Richmond, North Yorkshire DL10 4JN **Tel** (01748) 823571 **Evening meal** no **Prices** £££ **Rooms** 2 double; both have TV, radio, tea/coffee kit **Smoking** no **Credit cards** no **Children** no **Pets** no **Closed** never **Languages** French, Italian

---

Thoralby, SW of Leyburn

Low Green House

A classic small village in a classic Yorkshire Dale setting. Marilyn and Tony Philpott are experienced hosts, whose stone cottage offers homey comforts and rural views over the garden and the valley. Popular with walkers as well as sightseers.
Directions 8 miles SW of Leyburn. Get directions.

■ Thoralby, Leyburn, North Yorkshire DL8 3SZ **Tel** (01969) 663623 **Evening meal** yes **Prices** ££ **Rooms** 4 double; all have TV, radio, tea/coffee kit **Smoking** no **Credit cards** no **Children** yes **Pets** by arrangement **Closed** Christmas **Languages** English only

Yorkshire

York

Arnot House

This Victorian terrace house is on a quiet street, opposite the hospital grounds, and only a short walk from the Minster. Since 1995, Kim and Ann Robbins have redecorated, furnished rooms with antiques and recreated a Victorian ambience. Well priced. **Directions** off Bootham, the A19 to Thirsk. Get directions.

■ 17 Grosvenor Terrace, York YO3 7AG **Tel and Fax** (01904) 641966 **Evening meal** no **Prices** £££ **Rooms** 4 double; all have TV, radio, hairdrier, tea/coffee kit **Smoking** no **Credit cards** MC, V **Children** over 10 **Pets** no **Closed** Christmas **Languages** some French

---

York

Curzon Lodge & Stable Cottages

On a main road but backing on to the racecourse, Wendy and Richard Wood maintain high standards in the 17thC house and converted stables. The two-room suite is a bargain for four friends or a family. A short ride from the city on public transport. **Directions** 2 miles from heart of city. Get directions.

■ 23 Tadcaster Road, Dringhouses, York YO2 2QG **Tel** (01904) 703157 **Evening meal** no **Prices** £–£££ **Rooms** 8 double; 1 single; 1 suite; all have TV, radio, hairdrier, tea/coffee kit **Smoking** no **Credit cards** MC, V **Children** over 6 **Pets** no **Closed** Christmas **Languages** English only

---

York

Nunmill House

Russell and Cherry Whitbourn-Hammond's large Victorian house is well decorated, well priced and only a 10- to 15-minute walk from the city sights. Up a steep hill, with private and street car parking. Some four-poster beds; one family room. **Directions** S of heart of York. Get directions.

■ 85 Bishopthorpe Road, York YO2 1NX **Tel** (01904) 634047 **Fax** (01904) 655879 **Evening meal** no **Prices** ££ **Rooms** 7 double; 1 family; all have TV, hairdrier, tea/coffee kit **Smoking** no **Credit cards** no **Children** yes **Pets** no **Closed** Dec, Jan **Languages** English only

---

Late entries

Shortly before we went to press, readers suggested the following places to stay. They have not been inspected. Further reports are welcome. See details on page 32.

The Hall, Newton-le-Willows, Bedale, North Yorkshire DL8 1SW (01677) 450210. Glamorous Georgian home outside scenic village. Unusual oriental furniture. 3 rooms. ££££.

The North-West

Ash Farm

David Taylor, a former world amateur snooker champion, is now a professional. His 18thC stone farmhouse is deep in country, yet handy for Manchester and its airport. Luxury bedrooms, Janice's meals and a snooker table add to the attraction.
Directions 10 miles S of Manchester, off M56.

■ Park Lane, Little Bollington, Near Altrincham, Cheshire WA14 4TJ **Tel** (0161) 929 9290 **Evening meal** yes **Prices** ££–£££ **Rooms** 3 double; all have telephone, TV, radio, hairdrier, tea/coffee kit **Smoking** restricted **Credit cards** DC, MC, V **Children** over 9 **Pets** no **Closed** Christmas and New Year **Languages** English only

Poyll Dooey House

Thanks to the attraction of the Isle of Man's offshore banking, this secluded 18thC home, set in 2 acres of woodlands, has a steady stream of international guests. Expect a low-key, relaxed atmosphere. Light suppers available. A short walk to town.
Directions on edge of Ramsey. Get final directions.

■ Gardeners Lane, Ramsey, Isle of Man IM8 2TF **Tel** (01624) 814684 **Evening meal** yes **Prices** £££ **Rooms** 2 double; 1 single; all have hairdriers, tea/coffee kit **Smoking** no **Credit cards** no **Children** yes **Pets** no **Closed** never **Languages** English only

The Packet House

In Worsley Village, an affluent suburb of the city, Wendy Willett's mock Tudor home is actually 150 years old. Two rooms have attractive views over the canal. A useful base for business or pleasure, near both the airport and heart of the city.
Directions near Junction 13, M62. Get final directions.

■ 8 The Packet House and Boatsteps, Barton Road, Worsley, Manchester M28 2PB **Tel and Fax** (0161) 794 6167 **Evening meal** no **Prices** ££ **Rooms** 2 double; 1 single; all have TV, radio, hairdrier, tea/coffee kit **Smoking** no **Credit cards** no **Children** yes **Pets** yes **Closed** never **Languages** English only

Laburnum Cottage

Although the furnishing is rather bland, this is a businesslike base, convenient for Manchester and its airport. Rod Messenger is proud of his garden, which gives some character to this modern house. Breakfast is family-style, bedrooms are small.
Directions 18 miles S of Manchester. Get final directions.

■ Knutsford Road, Mobberley, Cheshire WA16 7PU **Tel & Fax** (01565) 872464 **Evening meal** no **Prices** ££ **Rooms** 3 double; 2 single; all have TV, radio, hairdrier, tea/coffee kit **Smoking** no **Credit cards** no **Children** by arrangement **Pets** no **Closed** never **Languages** English only

The North-West

Grove House

Handy for the ancient city of Chester, but set in a calm, walled garden, this spacious Victorian home makes a comfortable base. The multilingual Spiegelbergs do not offer dinner, but there are restaurants nearby. Well furnished and fairly priced.
Directions 5 miles E of Chester. Get final directions.

■ Holme Street, Tarvin, Cheshire CH3 8EQ **Tel** (01829) 740893 **Fax** (01829) 741769 **Evening meal** no **Prices** ££–£££ **Rooms** 2 double; 1 single; all have TV, tea/coffee kit **Smoking** restricted **Credit cards** no **Children** over 12 **Pets** no **Closed** Christmas, New Year **Languages** French, German, Italian

Knotts Cottage

This 250-year-old stone farmhouse, complete with thick beams, has a neat garden and views to the West Pennine Moors. Mrs Tolhurst was once a professional cook, so her hearty meals are praised. Old-fashioned comfort, including a snooker table.
Directions 13 miles N of Manchester. Close to M66.

■ Bury Road, Edgworth, Turton, Lancashire BL7 0BX **Tel and Fax** (01204) 852062 **Evening meal** yes **Prices** ££ **Rooms** 2 double; both have TV, tea/coffee kit **Smoking** restricted **Credit cards** no **Children** over 14 **Pets** no **Closed** never **Languages** English only

The Bower

Set in a designated area of natural beauty, The Bower is a relaxed family home. Sally-Ann and Michael Rothwell are keen bridge players; he also plays the piano and harpsichord. Nearby are coastal paths, a bird reserve, plus stately homes.
Directions near junction 35 of M6. Get final directions.

■ Yealand Conyers, Carnforth LA5 9SF **Tel** (01524) 734585 **Evening meal** yes **Prices** ££–£££ **Rooms** 2 double; both have TV, radio, hairdrier, tea/coffee kit **Smoking** no **Credit cards** no **Children** over 12 **Pets** by arrangement **Closed** never **Languages** Dutch

The Lake District and The North

Laurel Villa

Large and businesslike, Laurel Villa is in a Victorian terrace in the middle of town. William Morris designs add colour to the rooms; two have four-poster beds. The manager is Jenny Gittins. Rather expensive, but the private car parking is an advantage.
Directions Lake Road is part of one-way system. Get directions.

■ Lake Road, Ambleside, Cumbria LA22 0DB **Tel** (015394) 33240 **Evening meal** yes **Prices** £££–££££ **Rooms** 8 double; all have TV, radio, hairdrier, tea/coffee kit **Smoking** no **Credit cards** AE, MC, V **Children** yes **Pets** no **Closed** Christmas **Languages** some French

Demesnes Mill

This romantic watermill still has some original machinery and plenty of beams. Views of the weir and bird-life on the River Tees, yet on edge of historic market town.
Directions on river, across the Demesnes. Get final directions.

■ Barnard Castle, County Durham DL12 8PE **Tel and Fax** (01833) 637929 **Evening meal** no **Prices** £–££ **Rooms** 2 double; 2 single; all have telephone, hairdrier, tea/coffee kit; 2 have TV **Smoking** no **Credit cards** MC, V **Children** yes **Pets** no **Closed** Dec to Feb **Languages** English only

Middle Ord Manor House

Empty countryside and beaches contrast with Berwick's bloody history as a fortified border town. Joan Gray's 200-year-old home, with its walled gardens, lies beyond stone gates and up a drive. Comfortable without being luxurious: come here to relax.
Directions 3 miles W of Berwick. Get final directions.

■ Middle Ord Farm, Berwick-upon-Tweed, Northumberland TD15 2XQ **Tel** (01289) 306323; mobile (0585) 379280 **Evening meal** no **Prices** £££ **Rooms** 3 double; all have TV, radio, hairdrier, tea/coffee kit **Smoking** restricted **Credit cards** no **Children** no **Pets** no **Closed** Nov to Mar **Languages** English only

Tree Tops

Off the village green in East Ord, with woods and stream behind, the Nicholls' bungalow-style home is peaceful. John is Scottish, cooks Scottish dishes and even wears the kilt. Both rooms are comfortable with pretty furnishings.
Directions 2 miles west of Berwick. Get final directions.

■ The Village Green, East Ord, Berwick-upon-Tweed, Northumberland TD15 2NS **Tel** (01289) 330679 **Evening meal** yes **Prices** ££ **Rooms** 2 double; both have TV, radio, hairdrier, tea/coffee kit **Smoking** no **Credit cards** no **Children** no **Pets** no **Closed** Nov to Mar **Languages** English only

The Lake District and The North

East Mellwaters Farm

Anyone wanting to stay on a traditional working farm will be happy at Trish Milner's 17thC farmhouse, set in a valley amongst sprawling fields. Her evening meals, using lamb and beef from the farm, are served in a beamed kitchen.
Directions 6 miles W of Barnard Castle. Get final directions.

■ Bowes, Barnard Castle, County Durham DL12 9RH
Tel and Fax (01833) 628269 **Evening meal** yes **Prices** ££ **Rooms** 4 double; 1 single; all have TV, tea/coffee kit **Smoking** no **Credit cards** MC, V **Children** over 10 **Pets** no **Closed** mid-Dec to mid-Jan **Languages** English only

Toddell Cottage

Janet and Mike Wright left London, renovated this 17thC cottage and opened to guests in 1997. Cosy rooms; stylish, if small, bathrooms. Except for the house opposite, there is nothing within sight except a stream, sheep, fields and trees. A bargain.
Directions 10 miles W of Keswick. Get final directions.

■ Brandlingill, Near Cockermouth, Cumbria CA13 0RB **Tel and Fax** (01900) 828696 **Evening meal** yes **Prices** ££ **Rooms** 1 double; 1 family; both have TV, tea/coffee kit **Smoking** no **Credit cards** no **Children** over 5 **Pets** no **Closed** never **Languages** some French

Bessiestown Farm

Very much a working farm on the Scottish border, this is popular with families for overnight stops or longer holidays. Margaret Sisson's hearty welcome is matched by her breakfasts and well-priced dinners. The indoor heated swimming-pool is a bonus.
Directions 12 miles N of Carlisle. Get final directions.

■ Catlowdy, Near Longtown, Carlisle, Cumbria CA6 5QP
Tel and Fax (01228) 577219 **Evening meal** yes **Prices** ££ **Rooms** 4 double; 1 single; all have TV, radio, hairdrier, tea/coffee kit **Smoking** restricted **Credit cards** MC, V **Children** yes **Pets** no **Closed** never **Languages** English only

The Courtyard

The Weightmans restored this stone 18thC farmhouse, which overlooks the Tyne valley between Newcastle and the wild moorland. Expect flagstone floors and beams, with an eccentric mix of old furniture. The best bedroom has an ebony four-poster.
Directions 18 miles W of Newcastle. Get final directions.

■ Mount Pleasant, Sandhoe, Corbridge, Northumberland NE46 4LX
Tel (01434) 606850 **Fax** (01434) 606632 **Evening meal** yes **Prices** £££ **Rooms** 3 double; all have TV, tea/coffee kit **Smoking** no **Credit cards** no **Children** no **Pets** no **Closed** never **Languages** English

The Lake District and The North

Kendal

Holmfield

Brian and Eileen Kettle's Edwardian home in the Lake District is set in fine gardens, with a heated swimming-pool. The views of the fells and the castle are a bonus. Rooms are comfortable and tastefully furnished; breakfasts are enterprising.
Directions on private road off Kendal Green

■ 41 Kendal Green, Kendal, Cumbria LA9 5PP **Tel and Fax** (01539) 720790 **Evening meal** no **Prices** ££ **Rooms** 3 double; all have TV, hairdrier**Smoking** no **Credit cards** no **Children** no**Pets** no **Closed** never **Languages** English only

Lorton, W of Keswick

New House Farm

All alone on the valley road, this 17thC house belongs to John and Hazel Hatch and their young family. Bedrooms are named after their stunning views: Low Fell, Whiteside, Swinside. Busy in season when lunches and teas are served in the attractive barn.
Directions 9 miles W of Keswick. Get final directions.

■ Lorton, Cockermouth, Cumbria CA13 9UU **Tel and Fax** (01900) 85404 **Evening meal** yes **Prices** £££ **Rooms** 3 double; all have hairdrier, tea/coffee kit **Smoking** no **Credit cards** no **Children** over 12 **Pets** by arrangement **Closed** Christmas **Languages** English only

Natland, S of Kendal

Higher House Farm

Val Sunter is a charming, unflappable hostess whose 17thC house is on the edge of the village. Composers and professors come for the tranquility; walkers and sightseers for the practical, comfortable, fairly-priced bedrooms. Patio and large garden.
Directions 1 mile S of Kendal. Get final directions.

■ Oxenholme Lane, Natland, Kendal, Cumbria LA9 7QH **Tel** (015395) 61177 **Fax** (015395) 61520 **Evening meal** yes **Prices** ££ **Rooms** 3 double; all have TV, radio, hairdrier, tea/coffee kit **Smoking** no **Credit cards** no **Children** no **Pets** by arrangement **Closed** Christmas **Languages** English only

Portinscale, W of Keswick

Derwent Cottage

Major extensions in Victorian and Edwardian days transformed an 18thC cottage into this large, comfortable house. Book well ahead, since Mike and Sue Newman have a long list of regulars. Drying facilities for walkers; four-course dinners; mature garden.
Directions 1 mile W of Keswick. Get final directions.

■ Portinscale, Keswick, Cumbria CA12 5RF **Tel** (017687) 74838 **Evening meal** yes **Prices** £££ **Rooms** 5 double; all have TV, radio, hairdrier, tea/coffee kit **Smoking** no **Credit cards** MC, V **Children** over 12 **Pets** no **Closed** Nov to Feb **Languages** English only

The Lake District and The North

Tullythwaite House

The quiet Lyth Valley has a softer look than other parts of the Lake District. Hidden down a narrow country lane, Ian and Marie Parker's Georgian house has a large garden and spacious bedrooms. They serve their own honey at breakfast.

Directions 3 miles W of Kendal. Difficult to find. Get directions.

■ Underbarrow, Near Kendal, Cumbria LA8 8BB **Tel** (015395) 68397 **Evening meal** yes **Prices** ££ **Rooms** 3 double; all have TV, tea/coffee kit **Smoking** restricted **Credit cards** no **Children** over 10 **Pets** by arrangement **Closed** Dec, Jan **Languages** some French

The Archway

Windermere is full of bed-and-breakfasts but we like The Archway's quality of furnishings, its side-street location and the views of Coniston and the Langdales. Aurea and Anthony Greenhalgh are known for fine food: home-made bread, traditional English desserts.

Directions College Road is off Main Road. Get directions.

■ 13 College Road, Windermere, Cumbria LA23 1BU **Tel** (015394) 45613 **E-mail** archway@btinternet.com **Evening meal** yes **Prices** £££ **Rooms** 4 double; all have telephone, TV, radio, tea/coffee kit **Smoking** no **Credit cards** AE, MC, V **Children** over 10 **Pets** no **Closed** never **Languages** English only

Scotland

Birkwood Lodge

The Thorburns' unpretentious Victorian cottage is on a quiet, fir-lined side street. The bedrooms at the front have a view of the village green where the Highland Games are held in early August. Elizabeth's well-priced evening meals are a bonus.
Directions 11 miles W of Banchory.

■ Gordon Crescent, Aboyne, Aberdeenshire AB34 5HJ **Tel** (013398) 86347 **Evening meal** yes **Prices** ££ **Rooms** 3 double; all have TV, tea/coffee kit **Smoking** restricted **Credit cards** no **Children** yes **Pets** no **Closed** never **Languages** French, some Spanish

Cosses Country House

Deep in Robert Burns country, with golf courses nearby, this rambling white house has been home to the Crosthwaites for a decade. Here, comfort is a priority, home-cooked food a passion. Choose the suites in the converted stables for extra privacy.
Directions 18 miles N of Stranraer. Get final directions.

■ Ballantrae, Ayrshire KA26 0LR **Tel** (01465) 831363 **Fax** (01465) 831598 **E-mail** 100636.1047@compuserve.com **Evening meal** yes **Prices** £££–££££ **Rooms** 3 suites; all have TV, radio, hairdrier, tea/coffee kit **Smoking** no **Credit cards** MC, V **Children** yes **Pets** no **Closed** Christmas, New Year **Languages** English only

The Old West Manse

Popular with fly-fishers and golfers, the Taylors' home is up a steep driveway, which could be a little awkward for older visitors. Despite the Victorian theme to the 150-year-old house, all modern comforts are here, plus a hearty Scottish breakfast.
Directions on western edge of village, off A93.

■ 71 Station Road, Banchory, Kincardineshire AB31 5UD **Tel and Fax** (01330) 822202 **Evening meal** yes **Prices** ££ **Rooms** 3 double; all have TV, radio, hairdrier, tea/coffee kit, trouser press **Smoking** restricted **Credit cards** MC, V **Children** yes **Pets** yes **Closed** never **Languages** some French

Village Guest House

Rosalind Holmes deserves the fine reputation she has built in a short time. Her 18thC home is a few steps from the High Street. Our inspector, who stayed in the separate cottage in the garden, enjoyed an Aberdeen kipper for his breakfast. Very friendly.
Directions in middle of village.

■ 83 High Street, Banchory, Kincardineshire AB31 3TJ **Tel** (01330) 823307 **Evening meal** no **Prices** ££ **Rooms** 3 double; all have TV, hairdrier, tea/coffee kit **Smoking** no **Credit cards** no **Children** yes **Pets** no **Closed** never **Languages** English only

Scotland

Boat of Garten, NE of Aviemore

Heathbank

Crammed with bric-a-brac from all over the world, this Victorian house is best known for the first-class cooking of professional chef Graham Burge. Bedrooms are bold, perhaps with an African theme or black bathroom. Well-priced, well-organized.

Directions 8 miles NE of Aviemore on main street of village.

■ Boat of Garten, Inverness-shire PH24 3BD **Tel and fax** (01479) 831234 **Evening meal** yes **Prices** ££–£££ **Rooms** 7 double; all have hairdrier, tea/coffee kit **Smoking** no **Credit cards** no **Children** over 12 **Pets** no **Closed** Nov to Easter, but open New Year **Languages** French

---

Callander

Brook Linn Country House

Although rooms in this 150-year-old mansion are huge, decoration is plain, in stark contrast to the stunning views to the Trossachs. Fiona and Derek House, who are passionate gardeners, serve one of the best-priced meals in the area.

Directions house is on edge of village. Get final directions.

■ Leny Feus, Callander, Perthshire FK17 8AU **Tel and Fax** (01877) 330103 **Evening meal** yes **Prices** ££ **Rooms** 7 double; 1 single; all have TV, radio, hairdrier, tea/coffee kit **Smoking** no **Credit cards** no **Children** yes **Pets** by arrangement **Closed** mid-Nov to mid-Mar **Languages** French, German

---

Callander

Leny House

Play the Scottish laird in your own private glen. Alan and Frances Roebuck's historic stone manor looks like a Victorian shooting lodge, with tartan carpeting and antlers on the walls. Unpretentious and informal, with notably large rooms.

Directions 1 mile north of Callander. Get final directions.

■ Leny Estate, Callander, Perthshire FK17 8HA **Tel and Fax** (01877) 331078 **Evening meal** no **Prices** ££££ **Rooms** 4 double; all have tea/coffee kit **Smoking** no **Credit cards** MC, V **Children** yes **Pets** yes **Closed** mid-Oct to Easter **Languages** English only

---

Edinburgh

17 Abercromby Place

Lawyer Eirlys Lloyd's 200-year-old house still feels ultra-homey despite its size (five floors plus a coach house at the rear). Although family antiques abound, some parts need freshening up. In a quiet Georgian terrace. Private parking is a bonus.

Directions Abercromby Place is 3 streets N of Princes Street.

■ 17 Abercromby Place, Edinburgh EH3 6LB **Tel** (0131) 557 8036 **Fax** (0131) 558 3453 **Evening meal** yes **Prices** ££££ **Rooms** 6 double; all have telephone, TV, radio, hairdrier, tea/coffee kit **Smoking** no **Credit cards** MC, V **Children** over 12 **Pets** no **Closed** never **Languages** some French

Scotland

---

27 Heriot Row

The chintz, cerise walls and Adam fireplace in this 200-year-old Georgian town house are straight out of the pages of a glossy magazine. The Targett-Adams' taste and prices ensure comfort but the only car parking available is on the street.
Directions Heriot Row is three streets from Princes Street.

■ 27 Heriot Row, Edinburgh EH3 6EN **Tel and Fax** (0131) 220 1699 **E-mail** t.a.@cableinet.co.uk **Evening meal** yes **Prices** £££–££££ **Rooms** 2 double; 1 single; all have telephone, TV, radio, hairdrier, tea/coffee kit **Smoking** no **Credit cards** MC, V **Children** yes **Pets** yes **Closed** never **Languages** French, German, Italian, Spanish

---

Elmview

Glengyle Terrace is not the most elegant in New Town, but Mrs Marny Hill has comfortable, modern rooms in her basement which look out on a well-tended rockery. Guests have their own entrance and key to come and go. Thoroughly professional.
Directions Glengyle Terrace is NW of Princes Street.

■ 15 Glengyle Terrace, Edinburgh EH3 9LN **Tel** (0131) 228 1973 **Fax** (0131) 622 3271 **E-mail** elmview@cableinet.co.uk **Evening meal** no **Prices** ££££ **Rooms** 3 double; all have telephone, TV, radio, hairdrier, tea/coffee kit **Smoking** no **Credit cards** MC, V **Children** no **Pets** no **Closed** never **Languages** French

---

Twenty London Street

In the heart of New Town, George Birrell took over this elegant apartment in an 18thC town house in 1998. Bedrooms overlook gardens and have extras such as irons and small fridges. On-street parking only.
Directions London Street is a few minutes N of Princes Street.

■ 20 London Street, Edinburgh EH3 6NA **Tel** (0131) 557 0216 **Fax** (0131) 556 6445 **E-mail** gloriasplace@cableinet.co.uk. **Evening meal** no **Prices** £££–££££ **Rooms** 3 double; all have telephone, TV, radio, hairdrier, tea/coffee kit **Smoking** no **Credit cards** MC, V **Children** no **Pets** no **Closed** Christmas **Languages** French, Italian, Spanish

---

Ashburn House

Mrs Henderson is from a hotel-keeping family so runs a tight ship. Her passion for things Victorian include swags and drapes. Extensive Highland breakfasts include haggis and kippers.
Directions on corner of Achintore Road and Ashburn Lane.

■ Achintore Road, Fort William, Inverness-shire PH33 6RQ **Tel & Fax** (01397) 706000 **Evening meal** no **Prices** £££–££££ **Rooms** 4 double; 3 single; all have TV, radio, hairdrier, tea/coffee kit **Smoking** no **Credit cards** MC, V **Children** yes **Pets** no **Closed** Dec, Jan **Languages** French

Scotland

Galashiels

Binniemyre

A useful base for touring the Borders, this is a typical Scottish Victorian house. Despite features such as the original staircase and large rooms, it looks rather gloomy, though it does boast a billiard room. Carol Murray started serving dinner in 1997.
Directions on south side of town. Abbotsford Road is off A7.

■ Abbotsford Road, Galashiels, TD1 3JB **Tel and Fax** (01896) 757137 **Evening meal** yes **Prices** ££ **Rooms** 5 double; all have TV, radio, tea/coffee kit, trouser press **Smoking** no **Credit cards** MC, V **Children** yes **Pets** yes **Closed** Dec, Jan **Languages** English only

---

Grantown-on-Spey

Ardconnel House

One of several prim granite bed-and-breakfasts on this street, Ardconnel has large, well-furnished rooms. The decoration is less fussy than in many Victorian homes. Barbara Bouchard's dinners are attractively priced, and served at separate tables.
Directions house is in residential area, SW of town.

■ Woodlands Terrace, Grantown-on-Spey, Morayshire PH26 3JU **Tel and Fax** (01479) 872104 **Evening meal** yes **Prices** £££ **Rooms** 6 double; all have TV, tea/coffee kit **Smoking** no **Credit cards** MC, V **Children** over 10 **Pets** no **Closed** Nov, Dec **Languages** French

---

Inverness

Millwood House

Very much a private house in the residential part of Inverness, the 'capital of the Highlands'. The Lee family puts the emphasis on comfort and informality. Big communal breakfasts; pubs and restaurants for evening meals are within walking distance.
Directions house is on edge of town. Get final directions.

■ 36 Old Mill Road, Inverness IV2 3HR **Tel** (01463) 237254 **Fax** (01463) 719400 **E-mail** Millwood@sigma96.demon.co.uk **Evening meal** yes **Prices** £££ **Rooms** 2 double; all have TV, tea/coffee kit **Smoking** no **Credit cards** no **Children** no **Pets** no **Closed** never **Languages** English only

---

Islay, Hebrides

Kilmeny Farmhouse

Famous for the distinctive flavour of its whisky, Islay offers remoteness and peace. Kilmeny is a plain, white house with grander-than-usual furnishings for a working farm. Margaret and Blair Rozga deserve their high reputation for fine food.
Directions 4 miles from Port Askaig ferry. Get final directions.

■ Ballygrant, Isle of Islay, Argyll PA45 7QW **Tel and Fax** (01496) 840668 **Evening meal** yes **Prices** ££££ DB&B **Rooms** 3 double; all have TV, radio, hairdrier, tea/coffee kit, iron **Smoking** no **Credit cards** no **Children** over 12 **Pets** yes **Closed** never **Languages** Gaelic

Scotland

Jedburgh

The Spinney

Not many hosts truly welcome children but Mrs Fry does, and encourages them to play in the well-kept garden. Inside her long, low house, everything is equally neat and tidy, and bedrooms have recently been redecorated. Well priced.
Directions house is on A68, 2 miles S of Jedburgh.

■ Langlee, Jedburgh, Roxburghshire TD8 6PB **Tel** (01835) 863525 **Fax** (01835) 864883 **E-mail** Graham.A.Fry@btinternet.com
Evening meal no **Prices** ££ **Rooms** 3 double; all have TV, radio, hairdrier, tea/coffee kit **Smoking** no **Credit cards** MC, V **Children** yes **Pets** yes **Closed** Nov to Mar **Languages** English only

---

Jedburgh

Willow Court

This is a peaceful, unpretentious cottage overlooking Jedburgh. While not as historic as some, it is fresh-looking and airy, with modern bathrooms. Michael McGovern is a former amateur jockey with several trophies; his wife, Jane, is a good cook.
Directions house is near main market square.

■ The Friars, Jedburgh, Roxburghshire TD8 6BN **Tel** (01835) 863702 **Fax** (01835) 864601 **Evening meal** no **Prices** ££ **Rooms** 4 double; all have TV, hairdrier, tea/coffee kit **Smoking** no **Credit cards** no **Children** yes **Pets** yes **Closed** never **Languages** English only

---

Oldmeldrum, NW of Aberdeen

Cromlet Hill

Oldmeldrum is an attractive old town 30 mins from Aberdeen. Former geologist John Page has restored his Georgian mansion to its former glory; his wife, Isabel, deserves the credit for the fine garden. Well-placed for sightseeing and golf courses.
Directions 21 miles NW of Aberdeen. Get final directions.

■ South Road, Oldmeldrum, Aberdeenshire AB51 0AB **Tel** (01651) 872315 **Fax** (01651) 872164 **Evening meal** yes **Prices** ££-£££ **Rooms** 3 double; all have telephones, TV, tea/coffee kit **Smoking** restricted **Credit cards** no **Children** yes **Pets** no **Closed** never **Languages** English only

---

Late entries

Shortly before we went to press, readers suggested the following places to stay. They have not been inspected. Further reports are welcome. See details on page 32.

Dunfermline House, Melrose, Borders TD6 9LB (01896) 822148. Near the famous abbey, small rooms, warm welcome. 5 rooms. ££.

Index

Index

Index

Index

Index of place names

Index

Index

Index

Photo credit
p 52 Richard Greenly

Special Offer

Buy your **Charming Small Hotel Guide** by post directly from
the publisher and you'll get a worthwhile discount.*

Titles available:	Retail price	Discount price
Austria	£9.99	**£8.50**
Britain & Ireland	£9.99	**£8.50**
Britain: Most Distinctive Bed & Breakfasts	£9.99	**£8.50**
USA: Florida	£9.99	**£8.50**
France	£9.99	**£8.50**
France: *Bed & Breakfast*	£8.99	**£7.50**
Germany	£9.99	**£8.50**
Italy	£9.99	**£8.50**
USA: New England	£8.99	**£7.50**
Paris	£9.99	**£8.50**
Southern France	£9.99	**£8.50**
Spain	£9.99	**£8.50**
Switzerland	£9.99	**£8.50**
Tuscany & Umbria	£9.99	**£8.50**
Venice	£9.99	**£8.50**

Also available: Duncan Petersen's **Versatile/ Travel
Planner & Guides:** outstanding all-purpose travel guides.

Titles available:	Retail price	Discount price
Australia	£12.99	**£10.50**
California	£12.99	**£10.50**
Central Italy	£12.99	**£10.50**
Florida	£12.99	**£10.50**
France	£12.99	**£10.50**
Greece	£12.99	**£10.50**
Italy	£12.99	**£10.50**
Spain	£12.99	**£10.50**
Thailand	£12.99	**£10.50**
Turkey	£12.99	**£10.50**
England & Wales *Walks Planner &Guide*	£12.99	**£10.50**

Please send your order to:

Book Sales, Duncan Petersen Publishing Ltd,
31 Ceylon Road, London W14 OPY

*enclosing: 1) the title you require and number of copies
2) your name and address 3) your cheque made out to:*
Duncan Petersen Publishing Ltd
*Offer applies to UK only.

CHARMING SMALL HOTEL GUIDES

Would you like to receive information about special discounts at hotels in the *Charming Small Hotel Guide* series?

Many of our hotels are offering big savings on standard room rates if you book at certain times of the year.

If so, send your name and address to:

*Reader Information
Charming Small
Hotel Guides*
Duncan Petersen Publishing
31 Ceylon Road
London W14 OPY

For more offers see page 191